THE GOODIES'
criminal
BOOK OF RECORDS

This book was produced by George Weidenfeld and Nicolson Ltd
11 St. Johns Hill, London SW11

Designed by Anthony Cohen

Terribly, Terribly, Boring and Dull
SOLICITORS

987, Short Lane,
London WC1

to:

Weidenfeld and Nicolson,
II St Johns Hill,
London SWII

Dear Sirs,

At the request of my clients, The Goodies, herein after
referred to as The Goodies, my clients, I am informing
you of certain actions arising out of the recent publication
of a recent publication recently published by you - namely
"The Goodies File."

On my clients' behalf, I must make it plain to you that
they were distressed and embarrassed by the publication
of scurrilous material, <u>all</u> of which is <u>forged</u>, and in any
case they meant to burn it all before anyone got their hands
on it.

Mrs Edna Tole, herein after referred to as a good for nothing
old rat-bag, the author of this libellous collection, has not
yet been contacted, as she has left the country, and is
currently believed to be the first woman president of Venezuela.
Therefore, the full responsibility must rest with you, and it
thus falls to me to inform you that my clients and myself
are going to do you for <u>Libel</u>!

Coo, you aren't half for it!

We await your reply with interest,

Yours

Norman Boring

N.I.Boring LL.B.,W.

Godwater, Norfull, Ripov, and Cheet
Solicitors

Blessthis House,
Letsby Avenue,
Seldham,
WILTS.

...and Dull,

Our ref: ppBG/LC/*I34
Your ref: N.Burtenshaw
Date: this seventh day of the fourth

Dear Terribly,Terribly,Boring and Dull,

<u>re: Your accusation of Libel against our client Weidenfeld
and Nicolson</u>

Many thanks for your letter, this one looks like quite a little
moneyspinner for us in the old advocacy business, so let's hope it
gets to court, and once it's there, here's to a long run! Yes, thanks
indeed for slipping this little package our way - things haven't been
too brisk lately, and what with one thing and another, well frankly it's
been damned difficult getting hold of the briefs.
Well, down to business.
You can tell your clients that W & N deny it all of course, and are
extremely distressed and embarrassed themselves at the allegations of
deception levelled against them by your clients, and that they have to
defend their good name etc., you know the sort of thing; but lay it
on with a trowel!
If we could ever find old Mrs Tole, the we'd get some jolly handy
publicity by springing her as a surprise witness, yours or mine, makes
no odds really. Anyway, we look forward to dragging this one out with you,
and by the way, shall I book a court or will you?

ever

B.

B.Godwater (Company Director)

POST OFFICE

TELEGRAM

Prefix. Time handed in. Office of origin and Service Instructions. Words.

No.

OFFICE STAMP

N122 1512 LONDON TELEX 65

WEIDENFELD AND NICHOLSON 11 STJOHNS HILL SW11 =

DEAR WEIDENFELD AND NICHOLSON THANKS A BUNCH STOP YOUR

HANDSOME CHEQUE GREATLY APPRECIATED STOP IT WILL DO

NICELY TO PAY FOR OUR BARRISTER WHEN THE CASE COMES UP

NEXT MONTH STOP NOW YOU HAVE SETTLED OUT OF COURT DOES

THAT MEAN THAT WE SHANT BE SEEING YOU AT THE TRIAL ?

SHAME STOP LOVE FROM = THE GOODIES +

Oliver Double-Egg, Sossidge, Bacon and Chipps

(Barristers at Law)

Underbed Chambers,
Lincoln's Inn Fields,
London WC2

a few days later

Terribly, Terribly, Boring and Dull,
987 Short Lane,
London WCI

Dear Norman Boring,

We acknowledge the reciept of your letter of the 23rd inst., and shall
be only too pleased to represent you clients The Goodies in their
forthcoming action. We should arrange a meeting soon. You can find
us at the Inns of Court - usually The Pig and Whistle or The Pickled
Gibbon around the corner. Incidentally, I like the sound of your
surprise witness, if we can find her.

The case is to be heard early in the next Petty session, or possibly
the next Piddling Little session, or even Rather Unimportant session.
It is to be tried in front of Mr Justice I. Thort, which should be in
our favour, as he is inclined to be more lenient than Judge Foryor-Self.

P.T.O

Change of Address

Please note that as from April 12th
the new address of Edna Tole (Mrs).
formerly of 17, The Shed, Cricklewood,
will be

The Presidential Suite,
Simon Bolivar Centre,
Caracas,
Venezuela

THE TIMES April 24 1974
LAW REPORT
March 16 1975
Court of Appeal

Was Goodies File Fair Comment?

The Goodies v. Weidenfeld and Nicolson (Publishers).

Before Lord Luvaduck, Master of the Rolls, Lord Elpus, Keeper of the Buns, and Lord Justice Once, old joke.

The litigation here ensuing was first perpetrated by the aforesaid, on the peculiar grounds that, pending a claimant, albeit notwithstanding a fiduciary obligation, in so far as the basically untenable contingency would have claimed before proceeding to the prior commission which was not able to arrive at a satisfactory conclusion.

not understand a 'flippin' word he was talking about.

His Lordship then reminded the court of the precedent implied in the case of Desperate Dan v. The Beano (1948) in which the Cow Pie was seen to display three horns and a small thread of striped sweater believed stolen from Dennis the Menace.

Births

OCKHOMES
To Mr and Mrs Ockhomes, a daughter, Shirl.

TIMEWESAYGOODBYE-ICRYALITTLE
To Mr and Mrs Timewesaygoodbye-Icryalittle, a son, Avery

Adoption

UMMINMASSA
Mr and Mrs Umminmassa have adopted a small boy, Isaac.

Deaths

CHELSEA FC
Chelsea FC Passed away at Stamford Bridge on Saturday March 12th.

THE GOODIES v WEIDENFELD & NICOLS

First Day

"Anyone reading 'The Goodies File'" began Mr Brooke-Taylor, conducting the case for the Goodies, "would take us for a right load of loonies. We are consistently portrayed as thick as three short planks, behind the times, disreputable, clapped out, West Indian, and irresponsible."

Leaping to his feet, Mr Weidenfeld said he agreed with every word, except possibly "West Indian", and would prefer to substitute "Artful and Stingy". Mr Brooke-Taylor agreed to withdraw "West Indian", and accept "Self-Centred and Poofy instead." Mr Justice I. Thort said that he had just finished reading "the Goodies File" himself, and would like to add "Fat and Soppy" to the list.

The judge then reminded the Goodies since they were bringing the charge

it was up to them to refute these many allegations, and he suggested that Mr Brooke-Taylor might care to put 'West Indian' back in the list, as it was about the only one he could be fairly certain of disproving. There were, he said, some twelve insults at present on the list and, if the Goodies wished to go on with the case, they would have to prove that each one of them was unjustified.

He would be grateful if they would take them one by one and, if possible, in the order Mr Brooke-Taylor had delivered them. To this Mr Oddie replied: 'Gor blimey, if we have to answer that lot, it'll take another bleedin' book!' Mr Nicolson, leaping to his feet, exclaimed 'I'm glad to hear it, please may we publish it?' Contracts were then signed, and the court adjourned until tomorrow.

What's it all About, Edna?

This is Mrs Edna Tole, the ex-charlady who started it all by putting together The Goodies File. These are the questions we want answering now.

Is this book really — as Mrs Tole claims — "a searing social document exposing three of the greatest villains of our time"?

How can Mrs Tole now afford to live in a six-decked yacht in the Bahamas?

Can we make as much money out of screwing up the Goodies as Mrs Tole did?

What has happened to Chelsea?

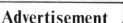

TOP SECRET FILE

Title *The Loony File*

THE GAARDIAN Thursday April 17 1975

LAW REPORT

Having established that the onus was upon Mr Brooke-Taylor acting on behalf of the plaintiffs, the Goodies, to answer each specific charge as made, the defence was asked to disprove the allegation that the plaintiffs were three "raving loonies." Spooking for the defence, Mr Book-Traylor called for a pysichartrts's report on himsefl and his colllllllllllleagues½½. "We ate certainly not roving leenies!" he explained to a lushed courtroot. "Nothig is father form the turth! Goob heavers, we are as sone as the next min!" The judye, asking for concrate edivence of their sanitory, denanded that the gentlemen of the jury be shown exhibit A – numely a comliation of ducoments qwert-yuiop to the Gooodies's's stoat of mined at (cont overloaf)

At this point the j...
tp point out tha...
were as "disr...
alleged, then th...
such glowin...
the presona...
in their Vi...
viz *exib¹*...
the Ju...
to mi...
case...

Goo...
next...
con...
den...
jur...
co...
yu...
m...

Sadly Mossed

Mrs Dora Smuth retires from the Guradian staff today, after 45 yaars service as chief proof-readre.

EXHIBIT A

SO YOU THINK YOU'RE A LOONY!?

Why not make up your mind one way or the other?
Remember, indecision can drive you nuts. It definitely is best to know about these things – then you can either capitalise on it (if people KNOW you're off your rocker you can get away with murder – literally! – You'll get invited to lots of parties, and, at the very least, you'll feel jolly important, 'cos everyone will stare at you).***

DR GRAEME GARDEN M.B. BsC.
(Ex. Parliamentary Candidate of the Loony Scientists Party- "IT TAKES ONE TO KNOW ONE"). All treatment is utterly confidential – honest! – if you don't believe us – just read Dr Garden's Book, 'Screwballs I have Known". W & N p.£3.20p.

OR You can decide to be cured. Either way,

DR GARDEN CAN HELP YOU

"LOO-NEE-
LOO-NEE"

DR GARDEN'S FUNNY FARM
(Door to door LOONY TESTING SERVICE)

LOONY TESTING
FREE

ALL YOU HAVE TO DO IS..
RING THIS NUMBER...
01-043 0012

OR

***
If you are extremely boring & normal — why not BECOME A LOONY? Dr Garden can arrange that too — send for details

and one of our vans will call discreetly DIRECT TO YOUR HOME. DR GARDEN will give you a thorough "LOONY TEST" in the comfort of *your* lavatory – AND it DOESN'T HURT A BIT.

If you already KNOW you're BARMY

I wish to visit
DR GARDEN'S FUNNY FARM
Please come & take me away in one of your little vans.
I shall/shall not need a straight jacket.
Name: _____ *I am over 18
Address: _____ & a nutter
Signed ....

DR GARDEN'S FUNNY FARM.

A secluded retreat in the heart of rural Cricklewood...

Where Dr Garden will...
Explore your past
Examine your frustrations
And take your money.

The Test is ABSOLUTELY FREE. Within 5 days you will receive DR GARDEN'S REPORT. If he considers you are NOT LOONY, you NEED pay ABSOLUTELY NOTHING – you CAN pay something if you like – or give him a present at least – but if you WANT to be a stingy sod – you NEED pay nothing.

OR if DR GARDEN considers YOU ARE A LOONY – you may decide to just accept it and, once again, you NEED PAY NOTHING – and our van will simply drive away, after circling your home for 2 hours blasting out its distinctive siren call of "LOO- NEE-LOO-NEE".

OR you may opt for treatment and a visit to

DR GARDEN'S FUNNY FARM*

These are completely UNSOLICITED TESTIMONIALS *(acceptable in lieu of payment).*

The 2nd pictures were taken within *one week* of entering DR GARDEN'S FUNNY FARM.

He can DO IT TO YOU...

BEFORE	AFTER
MR. A.	
Then; Artist & Sculptor	*Now;* Bankclerk

BEFORE	AFTER
MR. B.	
Then; World Famous Actor	*Now;* Chartered Accountant

BEFORE	AFTER
Mrs. C.	
Then; Housewife	*Now;* Prime Minister

OFFICIAL LOONY TEST

[Th]e object of this test is to decide whether or not you are a candidate for FUNNYFARM.
[Yo]ur answers will be treated in the strictest confidence, and what is more, no-one will
[se]e them except me - and of course, you. Owing to paper shortage, I have a limited supply
[of] questionnaires, and therefore, if more than one candidate is dwelling in the same
[ho]usehold, you may all use the same form. However, try not to be influenced by one
[an]other's answers, and please write in different coloured inks, so that I don't get
[co]nfused. You should not take more than 4 days over any question. Write in the spaces
[pr]ovided <u>only</u> and keep your answers short and to the point. If you do not understand any
[of] the questions, you are definitely a loony, and need not bother to complete the paper.

Dr. G. Garden.

WHAT IS YOUR NAME?

.. *Dr Graeme Garden*
.. *Tim Brooke-Taylor*
.. *& Bill.*

WHAT IS YOUR FAVOURITE COLOUR?

Blue
Green
Red

WHAT IS YOUR FAVORITE FOOD?

Vitamin C
Lobster Bisque, Steak au poivre with courgettes, pommes "Gratin Dauphinois" with Zabaglione to follow and an impertinent little bottle of Chateau Mouton Rothschild *Dinner*

WHAT IS THE MEANING OF LIFE? *State of ceaseless change and functional activity peculiar to organic matter.*

Don't know.

Do you mean this question existentially, temporarily or spiritually?

~~ARE YOU A LOONY?~~
WHAT IS YOUR OCCUPATION?

Smartiparts

Don't know.

Loony.

WHAT ARE YOUR AMBITIONS?
To rule the world.
To be Queen of England.
I should like to be able to stretch a piece of chewing gum out of my mouth for 34 inches, without it breaking & then roll it all back in with my tongue - still without breaking it.
AND
I'd like to be God. Please.

DO YOU HAVE ANY SECRET FEARS?

Yes, but I'm not telling cos they're secret.

I have a secret fear that a large man might kick me in the groin, beat me over the head with a mallet, and drill me full of bullets with a machine gun and it would hurt me very much. Also I wouldn't like to get drowned.

Nicholas Parsons.

THIS IS A FAMILIAR OBJECT SEEN FROM AN UNFAMILIAR ANGLE - WHAT IS IT?

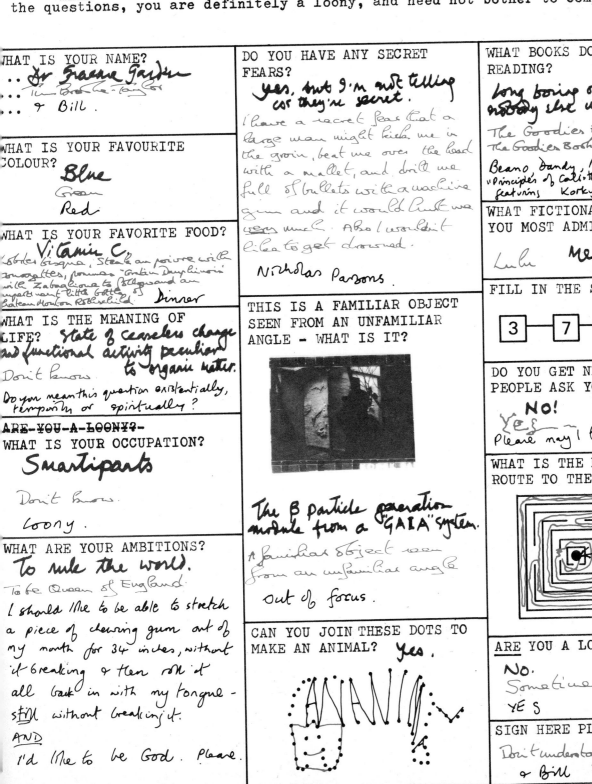

The β particle generation module from a "GAIA" system.

A familiar object seen from an unfamiliar angle

Out of focus.

CAN YOU JOIN THESE DOTS TO MAKE AN ANIMAL? *Yes.*

WHAT BOOKS DO YOU ENJOY READING?

Long boring ones that nobody else understands.

The Goodies File and The Goodies Book of Records.

Beano, Dandy, Reveille & Bechstein's "Principles of Calisthenics" (Illustrated Version) featuring Korky the Kat

---

WHAT FICTIONAL CHARACTER DO YOU MOST ADMIRE?

Lulu *Me* *Desperate Dan.*

FILL IN THE SPACE →

| 3 | 7 | 13 | ▓ |

DO YOU GET NERVOUS WHEN PEOPLE ASK YOU QUESTIONS?

NO!
~~*YES*~~
Please may I leave the room?

WHAT IS THE MOST DIRECT ROUTE TO THE CENTRE?

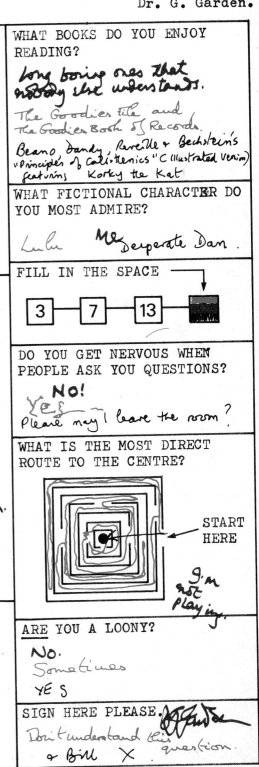

START HERE

I'm not playing.

ARE YOU A LOONY?

NO.
Sometimes
YES

SIGN HERE PLEASE. *[signature]*

Don't understand this question.
& Bill X

DR GARDEN'S FUNNY FARM.... TEST RESULT

Dear...Tim & Bill...... I am happy/regret to inform you that the result of y

Sub:...nothing; but please return the attached form to me.

"loony Test" shows that you are/are not a loony. Either way, you NEED pay

DR.D.G.GARDEN. G.

P.S. You will be pleased to hear that the test shows that I am/am not one to

---

Dear Dr. Garden,

*I wish to pay nothing. ✓✓

**I wish to enrol for one week's analysis and treatment at Dr Garden's

FUNNY FARM. ✓✓

Please tick your preference. ✓✓

SIGNED:.........Tim Brooke-Taylor...Bill.. X

(Bite along dotted line.)

Name of Pat

Date admitt

Results of

Peculiari

Intended

can hard

ridiculo

Genghis

Mr. Brooke

and the same goes for the

I intended to thoroughly examine their

fairly certain that traumatic experiences during the

to make them the pathetic cabbages they are today. I include my

evidence as a ready contrast to show what a non-loony is like.

PHASE 1 RESEARCH - INFANCY.   FORMATIVE YEARS.

Did the subjects like/dislike/know their parents? These adolescent portraits may well

give a clue.

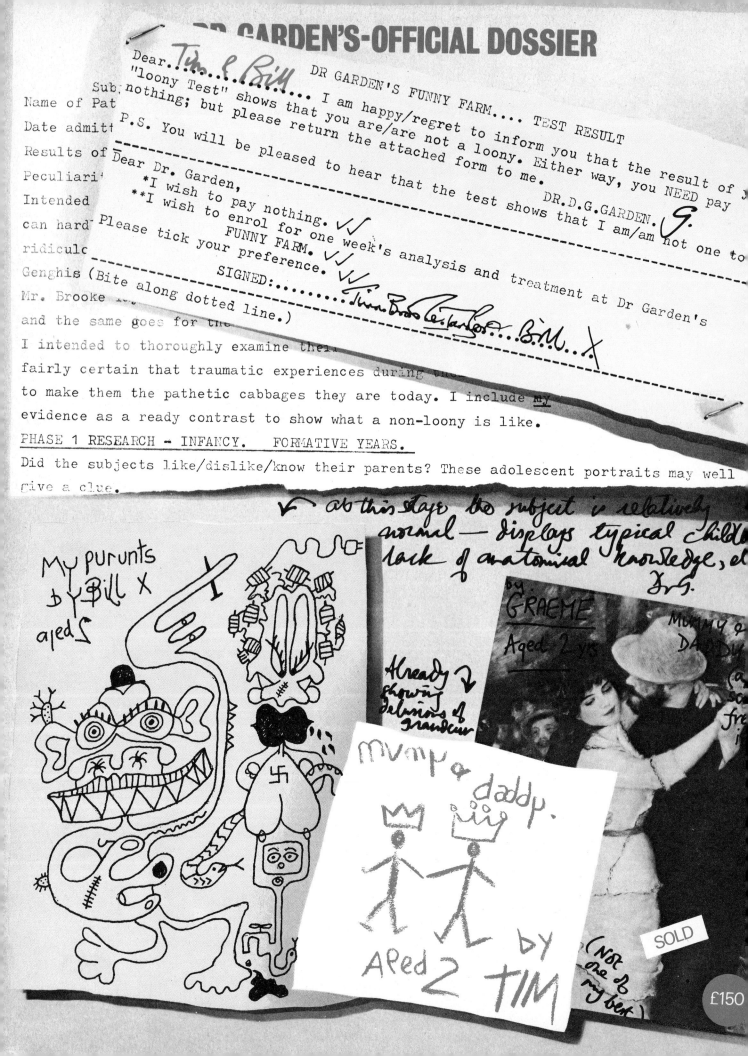

← at this stage the subject is relatively normal — displays typical child lack of anatomical knowledge, etc.

My purunts by Bill X aged 2

Already showing delusions of grandeur

by GRAEME Aged 2 yrs

MUMMY & DADDY

MUMY & daddy. aged 2 by TIM

(Not one of my best)

SOLD

£150

EARLY*
SCHOOL
REPORTS

-TAYLOR

tential ?
pressive ?
id he
never
os to
people ??

"THE KNOBS" KINDERGARTEN
(for the Sons of Smarmy Gentlefolk)

Patrons: Nicholas Parsons
Bamber Gascoigne

Name: T. Brooke-Taylor   Form: 1B (ints)
Age: 1yr. 2 mths   Average age of Form: 1yr. 2 mths.

Subject	Mark	Master's Comments
WALKING	C+	Not showing many signs yet, but he certainly is a right little crawler B.F
TALKING	B-	Booboo, gaga, gurgle gurgle O.J
DRESSING HIMSELF	C	Average - he tries hard but shows an unusual preference for mummy's clothes. D.F.B
POTTY TRAINING	B	His 'number ones' are amongst the most accurate in the class, but his No.2's inconsistent P.O.
TABLE MANNERS	A	Very nice. Will soon be ready for solids A.T.K
WIND	A+	Probably his best subject. He's full of it. Can "play" 'Land of Hope and Glory' from both ends! A.J.F.

General Progress: I find Timothy a slightly puzzling character. His speech trainer tells me that rather than ask for things, he just takes them, which shows commendable confidence in his social status. On the other hand, I believe he cries a lot, & I feel he would do well to control his emotions & adopt a slightly more mature attitude to problems. I'm sorry to hear about his problem with No. Two's, but I'm sure it need not hamper his public career.

Col. J. Streath
Headmistress

MR BROOK-TAYLORE

Early tendency to Exhibitionism.

See what he's wearing already!

ODDIE

NOTE:
WILD
EYES

'NERVOUS'
EARS

Aggressive
nose

GARDEN.

Wasn't I soulful?

The Epstein College of Advanced Techn...
(affiliated to the Nobel Assoc.)

Name: Graeme Garden   Form: Upper 6A
Age: 1yr. 9mths   Average age of Form: 18yrs 1mth.
1yr. 9mths

Subject	Mark	Professor's Comments
NUCLEAR PHYSICS	α+	Excellent. He has taught me a great deal P.ofE
BRAIN SURGERY	B+	What he lacks in accuracy he makes up for with enthusiasm promising C.K.
SPELLING	A.Q?	Week, in fakt, blody orfall J.F.P. A troublesome child-he insists on taking the subject seriously Dr.R.F
STINKS	CO₂	Three dimensional chess: excellent. Football: Poor. He must learn to walk Com.P.G
GAMES	A5	Quite astonishing

terribly !

H.M. OPEN ACADA
for
FOR YOUNG LOON

Name: Bill "Odd-ie"   No: 134AB
Age: 7 years 6 mths   Average ag

Subject	Mark	Warden's Comm
SEEING THINGS	A+	The most in visions of
MAX BYGRAVES IMPERSONATING	A++	Quite outstan
SQUEEKING	B-	Has tried hard this finger up thi
FALLING OVER	A	Very good. Hurt
ATHS	Z-	Poor
TING OUT LOONIE	A++	Excellent - ver
TICS	A+ ++	I feel he coul Prime Minis

During these important years we can witness the awakenings of sexual urges, fantasy tendancies etc. The subjects were prone to introspection and self-delusion perhaps. As do many teenagers, they all kept diaries, some pages of which are reproduced here – many of the entries are, I feel most significant and sometimes boring.

BILL ODDIE – Aged 15 — *N.B The Subject IN FACT looked like this* → *? LOONY*

PREFECTS' BALL 1956

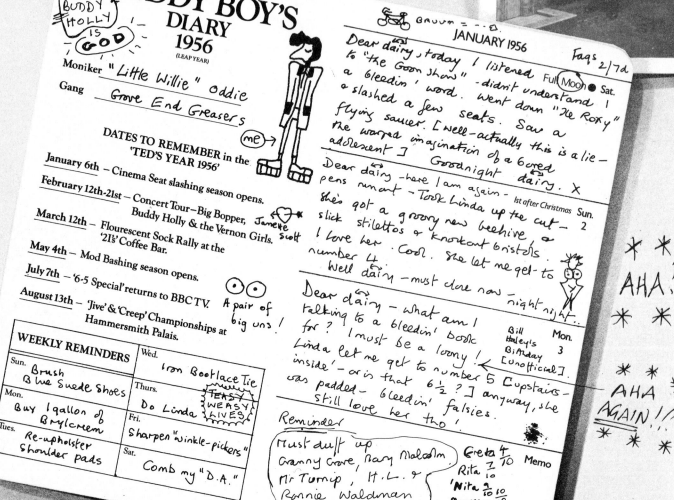

TEDDY BOY'S DIARY 1956
(LEAP YEAR)

BUDDY HOLLY IS GOD

Moniker "*Little Willie*" Oddie

Gang *Grove End Greasers*

me →

DATES TO REMEMBER in the 'TED'S YEAR 1956'

January 6th – Cinema Seat slashing season opens.

February 12th-21st – Concert Tour–Big Bopper, Buddy Holly & the Vernon Girls. *Janette Scott*

March 12th – Flourescent Sock Rally at the '2I's' Coffee Bar.

May 4th – Mod Bashing season opens.

July 7th – '6-5 Special' returns to BBC TV. *A pair of big uns!*

August 13th – 'Jive' & 'Creep' Championships at Hammersmith Palais.

WEEKLY REMINDERS	
Sun. Brush Blue Suede Shoes	Wed. Iron Bootlace Tie
Mon. Buy 1 gallon of Brylcreem	Thurs. Do Linda *TEASY WEASY LIVES*
Tues. Re-upholster Shoulder pads	Fri. Sharpen "winkle-pickers"
	Sat. Comb my "D.A."

JANUARY 1956

BRUM = ·Ø· *Fags 2/7d* *Full Moon ● Sat.*

Dear dairy, today I listened to "the Goon show" – didn't understand 1 bleedin' word. Went down "the Roxy" a slashed a few seats. Saw a flying saucer. [well–actually this is a lie – the warped imagination of a bored adolescent] Goodnight dairy. X

1st after Christmas Sun. 2

Dear dairy – here I am again – pens run out – Took Linda up the cut – she's got a groovy new beehive, slick stilettos & knockout bristols. I love her. Cool. She let me get to number 4 Well dairy – must close now – night-night...

Dear dairy – what am I talking to a bleedin' book for? I must be a loony! Linda let me get to number 5 – or is that 6½?] anyway, she was padded – bleedin' falsies. Still love her tho'.

Bill Haley's Birthday [unofficial] Mon. 3 *Upstairs*

Reminder
Must duff up Granny Grove, Mary Malcolm, Mr Turnip, H.L. & Ronnie Waldman

Greta 4/10 Memo
Rita 7/10
'Nita 9/10 10
Maureen 9/10
Noreen 9/10
P.S. I AM a deprived child.

Spi V5 *MUFFIN THE MULE IS AN OFFENCE*

AHA!! AHA AGAIN!!!!

CONTINUED OPPOSITE PAGE.

1956 JANUARY $\frac{CO_4 T 3\pi}{\times 2} \equiv \frac{1}{1st} \frac{1}{6}^{d}$ WEEK

JANUARY 1956

1 SATURDAY

Discovered Gamma Rays
(γ)

Read 'War & Peace' again

2 SUNDAY

Did open heart surgery
on Sir W. Churchill.
Satisfactory!

3 MONDAY

Clean so

4 TUESDAY

a.m. Split the atom.

p.m. Mended it again.

Not bad for a Tuesday.

5 WEDNESDAY

Day off. Wrote
Text-book on 'Pheromones'.

THURSDAY

Nobel Prize!
(Early closing.)

Notes

$= Mc^2$

NON-FANTASY

N.B- No
NASTY
SEXUAL
REFERENCES

NORMAL
TEENAGE
ACTIVITIES.

🧸🧸🧸🧸🧸🧸🧸🧸

The Baby TIM 's Diary   1955

(by ME (TIM)).

TUESDAY   My dearest darling diary,
Hello. Oh how my spirit flies — do you
mind if I tell you my secret love? I saw
HER today. Oh how my heart rings when
I look at her sensible shoes! Oh how I
long to lick them. I have composed a song
to HER   (To the tune of 'Carolina')

♫ Nothing could be finer ♫♫ (cherries)
Than Elizabeth Regina — in the mor-ning!

(There — I've told you. Hush now diary,
not a word to anyone — Don't even tell
Teddy)

Also watched 'the Interlude' (Angel Fish) and
Prudence kitten — was violently sick
Granny keeps farting   Sunny + warm
Well, must close — Night, Night.   X Tim

🧸🧸🧸🧸🧸🧸🧸

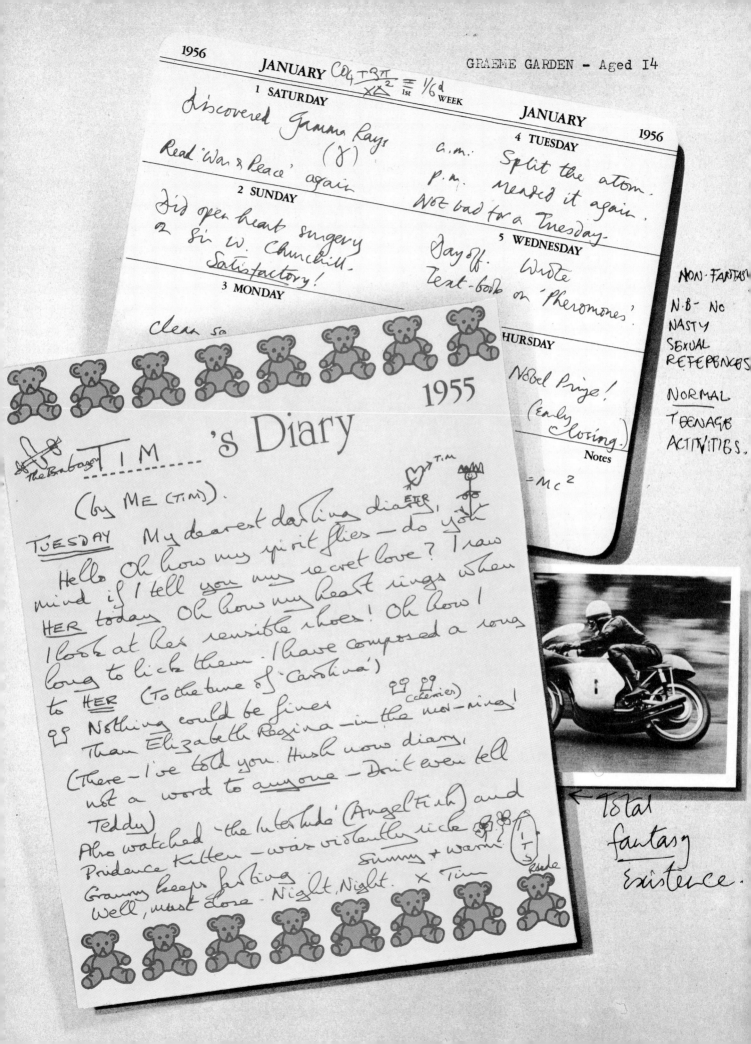

← Total
fantasy
existence.

PHASE 3 RESEARCH - EMOTIONAL STIMULI

Having studied the subjects formative years, it was becoming clear to me that two of
them were definitely emotionally disturbed. I now had to discover which two.

EXPERIMENT

A series of 6 stimulating images is shown to the subjects - a new picture every 3
seconds. A hidden camera records their facial reactions to the images. Their pulse
rate is also recorded.

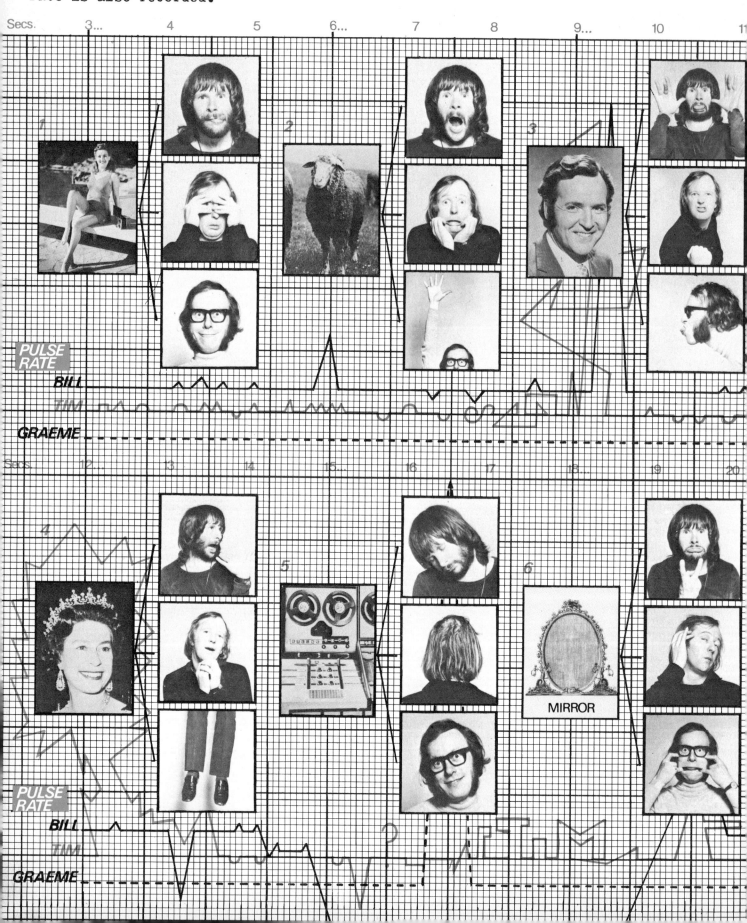

PHASE 4 RESEARCH ... THE SUBCONSCIOUS.

SLEEP AND DREAMS

It is often possible to tell whether or not a person is emotionally disturbed by
observing them whilst asleep (whilst THEY're asleep that is, not me. I mean, if
I were asleep, I wouldn't be able to observe them, would I? Anyway, why am I
explaining that to YOU? Cos YOU aren't going to read this file, cos its private
and secret and its mine, all mine, do you hear me? .. MINE! Hahahahaha! And I don't
need to explain it to MYSELF, do I? Cos I KNOW what I mean. Oh yes. I THINK I do.
Yes I DO. Anyway, where was I? Oh yes, the point is, you see...no, YOU don't see...
I see.... the point is , loonies often give themselves away during their sleeping
hours. For a kick off, they sometimes talk in their sleep, and if you're very lucky,
they shout out "I'm a loony". Not that you can believe everything loonies tell you.

Anyway.. I decided to observe the subjects sleeping habits.

1. What did they wear to go to bed in?

TIM: A "Union Jack" Nightie. Fair Isle Liberty Bodice. M.C.C. Tie,
     and   and "Lords Taverners" Centenary Bedsocks.

Tim likes his subconscious!
& Ready for adventure ?!

BILL: A suit of armour. Crash Helmet. Chain Mail socks
            and spiked running shoes. *(Hope he isn't going to have*

Bill — N.B. Afraid of his subconscious? that boring old dream about running away all the time.

ME (GRAEME): Normal Ex. Army Sterilised Polythene Piggy Jim Jams,
            and common or garden Jack boots.

And why not ?!

2. What did they take to bed?

TIM: A plastic O.B.E. A teddy bear(real one)

BILL: Half a brick. A fire extinguisher. And a machine Gun.

— NB: Bill is basically insecure. (He sleeps in a cast-iron box — locked from the inside.)

GRAEME(ME): Racquel Welch(Not a real one)

3. THEIR DREAMS

At 1200 hrs the subjects were fed with two pounds of cheese.
at 1300 hrs they fell asleep and I observed them as they dreamt. As is fairly
common, they often changed their sleeping positions. What did these postures mean??...

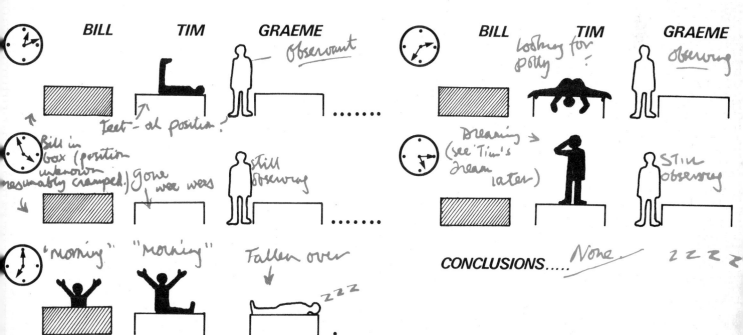

On waking, the subjects wrote down what they could remember of their dreams.

GRAEME'S DREAM

I didn't have a dream 'cos I was up all night observing the other two and I still
havn't ca ug t upp nd im getting very ovetiried ands inmnmnm 4~7-~~333~~222 fklim zzzzzzzzzzzz
zzzzzzzzzzzzzzzzzzzzzzzzzzzzzzzzzzzzzzzzzzzzzzzzzzzzzz

My horrid, rotten, stinking dream..dream? Soddin', bleedin' nightmare I'd say.
By Bill Oddie

First of all I was in this Glitter suit, only it wasn't so much a suit as a
jockstrap. And I was riding this whacking big motor bike, with a ruddy big
exhaust pipe, and I was being chased by all the girls from the Younger Generation
and Pan's People and the Three Degrees.
And then all of a sudden, Mary Whitehouse came tazzing up and overtook the lot of
them, and she was riding this horse....only it wasn't really a horse, it was
Lord Longford. And then she leapt off him onto my pillion, and my motor bike
turned into a hovercraft.
And then Lew Grade ran up and burst the hovercraft with his nose and it flew off
like a balloon (the hovercraft, not his nose) and I fell off and kept falling
and falling, until I landed in a huge pool of Elvis Presley's hair oil.
Then I got out and I was trying to climb up this cliff face... only it wasn't
a cliff, it was all pink and smooth and horrible, and it reminded me of
Nicholas Parsons' cheeks. And then I suddenly realised....it was Nicholas Parsons'
cheeks. And I kept sliding down them, 'cos there was no hairs, so I had nothing to
cling onto. But then, all of a sudden, he got his hanky out to blow his nose
and it all smelt of TCP and rose water; and anyway, he did blow his nose and he
stuffed me right up his left nostril.
It was all dark in there until suddenly a light came on and there was Eamon
Andrews, and he said "This is your life, Bill Oddie." And then suddenly I was on
the telly and it was 'This is your Life' and Eamon was saying "Do you recognize
this voice?" and I said "Yes, that's Crippen, a budgie I once had." Eamon said
"Yes, come in Crippen." and on came this budgie, only it wasn't a little budgie,
it was bloody enormous, and it wasn't Crippen at all, it didn't even have a
budgie's face, it had Tony Blackburn's!
It kept telling rotten jokes and saying "Who's a pretty boy, then?" And then
suddenly Eamon Andrews took his wig off and hundreds more budgies flew out and
they were all flipping Tony Blackburn, and they all kept telling jokes and
chattering, it was almost as bad as Radio One.
Then one of them picked me up and flew off with me, and then he dropped me, and
I was falling again, and I fell right down Vanessa Redgrave's cleavage. As soon as
I'd crawled out the other end, a spotlight came on and I'm perched, stark naked,
right on top of this one hundred foot flagpole with a great pool of crocodiles
underneath;;and Hughie Green shouts out "O.K. for you, Bill Oddie..Opportunity
Knocks." Then I start singing "I did it my way" and all the time I'm sliding
down this flagpole and one of the crocodiles opens his mouth and it's got these
ruddy great gleeming white teeth and suddenly I realize that it's not a crocodile,
it's Donny Osmond. I think he's going to bite my leg off; but it's worse than
that ....he starts to sing.
And that's why I woke up screaming, and I'm jolly glad that I took my half a
brick and my machine gun to bed with me; otherwise I'd have been really
frightened, although the fire extinguisher wasn't much use.

Anyway, now I'm quite looking forward to the next episode.
Night night.

love X Bill Oddie

DR GARDEN'S FUNNY FARM

FINAL REPORT

Having accumalated the mass of information herinforemost contained,
I was certain of one thing - I had no idea what I was doing. So I
fed the information to my lovely little computer.

COMPUTER ANALYSIS OF SUBJECTS:

Computer No. X4PZ2

Name of Loony BILL ODDIE

Comments FINDS THE WORLD UNBEARABY ANTAGONISTIC
BRUTAL AND HORRIFYING. TOTALLY AGREE WITH HIM.

Suggested Treatment WHY NOT JUST GIVE UP?

Computer No. X4PZ2 (BUT YOU CAN CALL ME LOLA)

Name of Loony TIM BROOKE TAYLOR

Comments A FRUITCAKE.. BUT ONE DAY HE MAY RULE
THE WORLD. HAVE NO WISH TO UPSET HIM.

Suggested Treatment GIVE HIM AN O.B.E.

Computer No. X4PZ2 (BUT YOU CAN CALL ME SWEETHEART)

Name of Loony DR. GRAEME GARDEN

Comments SURE, HE'S CRAZY - BUT I LOVE HIM BUT THEN
MAYBE I'M CRAZY TOO. WHO KNOWS??....

Suggested Treatment HOPELESS CASE RECOMMEND CARRERR IN
POLITICS - SCIENCE - TELEVISION

DR GARDEN'S FUNNY FARM

Job no. 237
Invoice: 15/98322.

Observing subject's

...RDEN'S FUNNY FARM

...cate of Non-Loonines

...ertify that TIM BROOKE-TAYLO...

...ny, and that anyone who says he...

...unch up the bracket from me.

...and this 12th day of April

Lola
Computer

Dr. J.G. Gard...
Dir. of Funny Farm.
Loony expert.

DR GARDEN'S FUNNY FAR...

Certificate of Non-Loonine...

I hereby certify that BILL ODDIE

is not a loony, and that anyone who says he is

will get a punch up the bracket from me.

Witness my hand this 12th day of April the year 75

6 bags of aniseed balls	1-30
3 large bananas	18p
2 straight jackets	5
Electric chair	200.
Batteries	0-
TOTAL:	£6, 34

Prompt payment will be appreciated.

ALL ABOUT COMPUTERS
BY GRAEME GARDEN

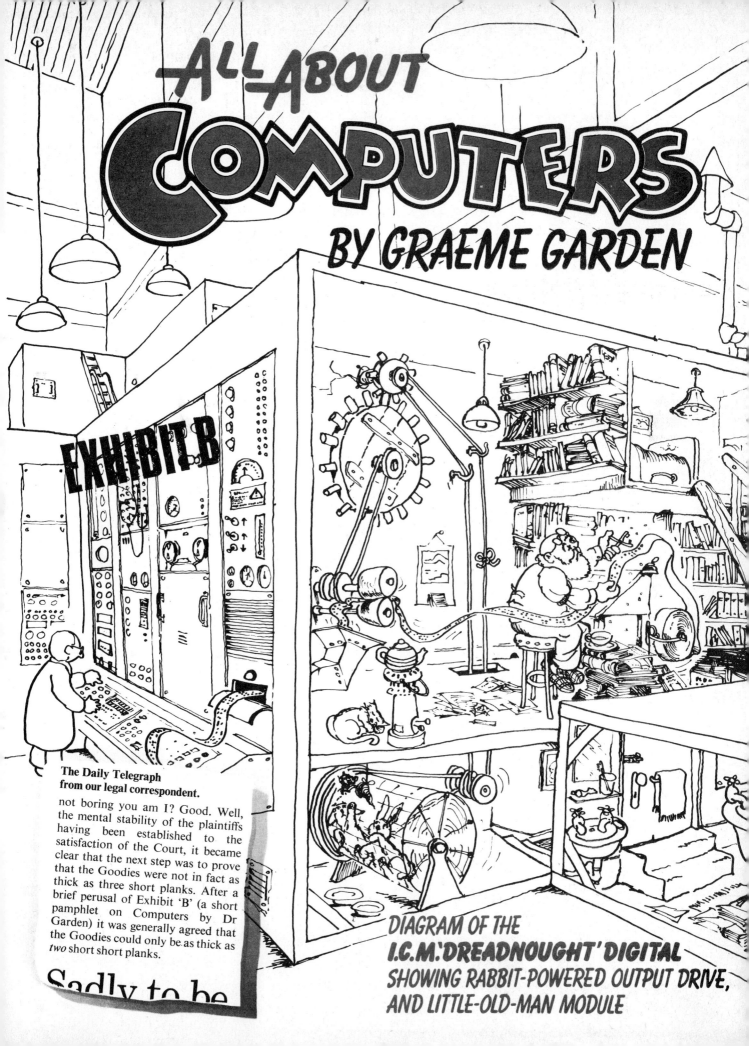

EXHIBIT B

The Daily Telegraph
from our legal correspondent.

not boring you am I? Good. Well, the mental stability of the plaintiffs having been established to the satisfaction of the Court, it became clear that the next step was to prove that the Goodies were not in fact as thick as three short planks. After a brief perusal of Exhibit 'B' (a short pamphlet on Computers by Dr Garden) it was generally agreed that the Goodies could only be as thick as *two* short short planks.

Sadly to be

DIAGRAM OF THE
I.C.M.'DREADNOUGHT' DIGITAL
SHOWING RABBIT-POWERED OUTPUT DRIVE,
AND LITTLE-OLD-MAN MODULE

How to build your own computer

You know, building your own computer is easier than you think. At least, it is if you think it's going to be pretty difficult. Then again, if you think it's going to be easy, then you might find it's more *difficult* than you think. All in all and not beating about the bush – if you think it's going to be reasonably easy but with difficult bits, then I'd say you'd got it about right. Anyway, if you want to go through with it – this is what you do . . .

Ingredients

You will need:–

a One stout box or case to enclose the works (or 'Hardware' as we computer experts call it).

b Some 'Hardware'.
Obtain, from a Hardware Shop, some transistors, printed circuits, mag. storage cores, astable multivibrators, binary counters, OR, AND, NOR, NAND gates, flip-flops, oscillators, numerators, comparators, integrators etc. etc. (You realise I'm not talking about **any** old hardware shop, right? Right.)

c Also you may need some solder, screws, wire, string, glue and stuff like that, available for a few pence from your local Computer Outfitters.

Instructions

Well here you are at last – ready to assemble your very own Computer. Just follow these instructions, and you'll find it all quite simple: always remember the basic rule–think *LOGICALLY!* If you do, then you'll find about

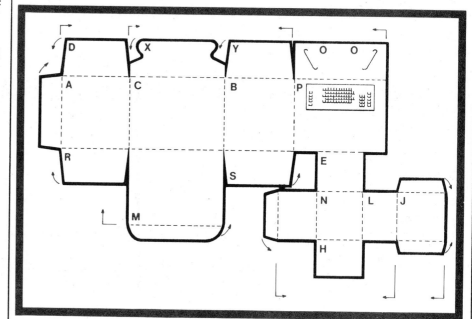

everything quite as easy as if you were easily doing anything at all the same in the easy and even logical things can become if you don't care for, so think *LOGICALLY!*

Assembling the case

a Trace the diagram (above) on to tracing paper.

b Trace it again on to another piece of tracing paper – JUST IN CASE! (This is known as a **back-up system.**)

c Once you have traced the diagram, carefully re-draw it at full-scale size on a large piece of tracing paper. It should come out at about 8 ft by 15 ft, so you are going to need a piece of paper, say, a bit bigger than 8 x 15 feet

square. That works out at 120 square feet, which is an unrealistic size for a piece of tracing paper really – so you'd better settle for maybe two 60 sq ft pieces glued together. (Four 30 sq ft pieces would do). Just remember, you need 1114·8364 square decimetres precisely. In other words, you ask for four pieces of tracing paper measuring 1·2162 by 2·286 metres. As a matter of fact, eight pieces measuring 60·81 centimetres by 1·143 metres would also suffice, as indeed would SIX pieces of tracing paper, 10·16 cm by 12·7 cm square, but only if joined together as shown below. (And it doesn't really have to be tracing paper.)

d Apologise to the man in the shop where you tried to buy the paper. Send him flowers perhaps.

e Copy the full size drawing on to a sheet of mild steel, $\frac{1}{4}$ in thick, and again 120 feet square. Or again you can glue together several smaller steel sheets, as in *c*.

f Cut out the shape from your steel plate, score the dotted lines with scissors, perforate slots, fold according to the arrows, and insert tabs. Your computer case is now complete.

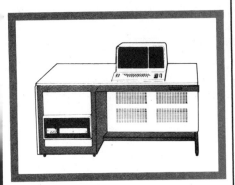

All you need to do now is to hire a welder to cut a big hole in the back so that you can put things inside it.

Assembly of the hardware

a REMEMBER! In the assembly of the Hardware (or as we Computer experts call it, 'the working parts') we shall be relying frequently on a material as old as the hills, or very nearly. Put it this way, it's probably as old as some hills, but not as old as most of them.
Got it yet? Well here's a clue: it begins with S and ends with tring. Yes, that's it, string. One of man's earliest inventions, yet still very much with us today, and in the field of computer manufacture, invaluable. Good old string, I say!

b Well, that's quite enough about string.

c Printed circuits.

d Yes, printed circuits. This is a printed circuit.

e And this is a piece of string. Notice the difference.

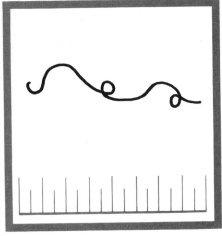

f Let's take another look at the printed circuit.

Rather appealing isn't it? You will note that the electrical impulse 'E' enters the circuit at input 'I', and is supposed to emerge at output 'K'. See if you can help E to find his way from I to K without crossing his own tracks – and can you find three hidden ice-lollipops in the picture?

g Look, when you've quite finished *fooling about*, let's get on with the job shall we?

h Trace the pattern of the Printed circuit on to a sheet of inert matrix covered with a conducting layer of copper film, then etch the pattern with Hydrofluoric Acid (careful!).

i That was only practise. So, when the burns have healed you can proceed to the next step.

j We live in an age of miniaturisation. Everything is getting smaller, and there's not much we can do about it so there you are. Anyway, your circuit must now be miniaturised, so just copy it once more on to a LSI silicon chip no more than 0·05

mm. in width.

k Never mind the excuses – get on with it!

l Come off it – you know as well as I do where to get a LSI silicon chip!!

m No! Not telling!

n Oh you've got one have you?

Right. Titchy, isn't it? Well, off you go, get your circuit copied on to it.

o Well done. And now that you've made your first micro-integrated circuit, it's all just plain sailing. Of course our computer will need more than one of these tiny circuits — we shall need three or four, maybe even FIVE thousand of them.

p Calm down.

q That's better. Well, now you can settle down to making five thousand of those little circuits. You know it didn't take you all that long to make the first one, and the second one shouldn't be quite so difficult . . .
Tell you what — why not make five thousand little marks, and then you can cross one off every time you finish a circuit, say, one every six months — *or even less!*

r After a while, pack it in.

Assembly of hardware: Phase two
a About five or six years later, you may find the bits and pieces of your unfinished computer, and you may think to yourself . . .
Did I give up too soon?
Should I have persevered?
Should I have soldered on?
Should I have tried harder to finish what I set out to do?

b No.

Assembly of hardware: Phase three
a A few short months after phase two, you are ready to commence phase three. Grit your teeth, and take the plunge — it is now time for:

The final assembly
Glue together the remaining parts, nail the integrated circuits in place (any place will do), tie the whole lot into a neat bundle with string, and *voila!*

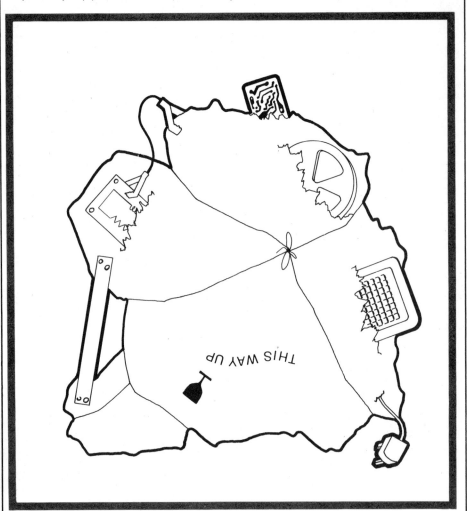

Your computer is complete!
Or at least nearly complete. After all these years you have probably lost the original case we made (remember?). But don't worry — you can easily find some sort of metal container which will do (see below). Just stuff your computer into it, leave it out on the pavement, and with any luck the dustmen should empty it on Wednesday.

TOP SECRET FILE

Title *The Case of "Cricklewood Man"*

EXHIBIT C

BRITISH MUSEUM FACES BANKRUPTCY

By our rather special
correspondent:

Blimey ! What next, I
 ~~~ ~bdnvh ,the good ~
 ~ sstish Museum
 ~ez, the red? But
 ~kcmz a true. Unle~
 ~d,sme attract mor~
 ~aldcns eight tour~
 ~dmcm ankhamu~
 ~one, you've seer~
 ~a all. The grav~
 ~ation n~

BRITISH   MUSEUM

(AS ADVERTISED ON T.V.)

Dear Goodies
        As you may hav
in recent press reports we
museum find ourselves i
creek without a paddle in
words financially embarr
to put it another way skirt
        What we need is ?
possibly you may help us i
really sensational find so
as exciting as the Piltdow
which through admitted
fake did us a lot of g
        P.T.O

THE GOODIES
No Fixed Abode, Nr. Cricklewood, London

Dear Curators of The British Museum,
        Thank you for your plea of the 9th of this
month.
        Fear not! The job's as good as done and the
plans are already afoot to provide you with
the sensation that we imagine you will
require.

CRICKLEWOOD MAN LIVES!!!

Yours,
        The Goodies

The Goodies

TIMES OF OLD

A GOODIES PUBLICATION

INSIDE THIS ISSUE

CRICKLEWOOD MAN SENSATION!

WEEK BY WEEK BUILDING UP A COMPREHENSIVE ENCYCLOPAEDIA OF ARCHAEOLOGY

Number 2

Dear Readers,

It is our firm belief that mankind can only look forward by looking back. Clearly, this is a very silly thing to believe, but there you are. Also, we, as Editors of this encyclopaedia – (building weekly into a comprehensive and impressive collection of Archaeological knowledge with which to clutter up your shelves and bore your friends but that's your problem and see if we care) – hope merely to bring you a hint of the excitement of delving back into the mists of time . . .

Sincerely,

The Goodies

The Goodies.

Britain LAND OF SECRET LEGENDS

BRITAIN is a land of Secret Legends. You may not have heard any of them, but that's probably because they are secret. Here we present just a few of these uncanny yarns . . .

THE STANDING MEN OF HOY

IN THE REMOTE ORKNEY ISLANDS, you can find a circle of large upright stones.

It is said that if you stand alone in the middle of the circle, stark naked, at sunset on Midsummer's Eve with one leg in the air, you will eventually see some men standing watching you. Sooner or later, one of the standing men will probably shout "Hoy! What's your game?"

THE HIDING GHOST of STRADDLING HALL

SIR HARRY STRADDLING was a shy man all his life – most of which he spent hiding from his friends and relations – even from complete strangers. The story goes that on his death-bed he vowed to return and hide from all those who visited Straddling Hall. Disbelievers may scoff, yet it is an uncanny fact that, since his death, Sir Harry's ghost has never once been seen . . .

How St. Albans Got Its Name

It was named after St Alban.

DIG THIS

HOT NEWS OF LATEST EXCAVATIONS
by DIGGER

GREETINGS, fellow Antique-Freaks!
And have I got news for you?!! Yes indeedy – cos latest news from *THE GOODIES* is that their *CRICKLEWOOD* dig has turned out to be a site for sore eyes! The lads have dug deep and come up with plenty! The final success of their labours remains to be seen – and some of the remains to be seen are shown below – vouched for and reconstructed by experts at the British Museum. Wow!

BRITISH   MUSEUM

REPORT ON EXCAVATION: Cricklewood Site.

POTTERY FRAGMENT shown left, believed to date from between 2 to 2½ million years BC. Probably remains of a primitive type of pottery helmet, or ceremonial hat. Artist's reconstruction (left)

THE VENUS OF CRICKLEWOOD.
This battered relic (left) reveals that Cricklewood Man, Primitive though he was, had some skill in working metals – in this case to produce a crude representation of a female figure, for use no doubt in some from of worship. Artists reconstruction (left).

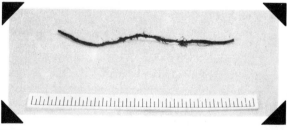

PRIMITIVE STRING discovered at the site, measuring six inches in length suggests that these finds may date back further than the Bronze, Iron, or even Stone Age – indeed Cricklewood may have been the very birthplace of String-Age Man! It is more than possible that string was actually invented at this location as long ago as 2,000,794 years BC, say in August, could be a Wednesday, probably rather late in the afternoon.

EARLY WOOD CARVING, thought to represent a grotty old bit of stick. Very realistic.

A RARE FIND – what could be the earliest ruler ever unearthed. It is the same length as this bit of string.

YIKES! Those fellas sure know their stuff! That's all for now, but I'll be back next issue with more pots and puns! See you later, excavator!

Digger

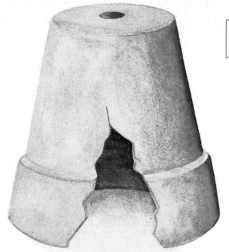

"The Cricklewood DWELLING"

POSSIBLE CLUE TO MAN'S EARLIEST SETTLEMENT?
by Anne Tiquity.

TIM BROOKE-TAYLOR wiped the sweat of the morning's labours from his assistant's brow, and sank on to the camp stool next to the rather pansy table. A hard day's work had taken its toll. "Phew!" he murmured, "I'm knackered."

We were sitting in the makeshift headquarters of the Goodies' famous Cricklewood Site, which had already yielded so many rich finds, and was beginning to make Archaeologists think twice about their cherished theories. It was the richest of these discoveries that I had come to see.

"I have in my hand" said Tim Brooke-Taylor, "what is possibly the most important find of recent years. This fragile piece of earthenware could revolutionise our concept of primitive man's social development. It is impossible to estimate the significance of this delicate specimen. Here – catch!"

Breathless, I examined the object he had thrown me. A small, reddish clay structure – circular with sloping walls and a hole in the top, and a crude opening in one side. It was thrilling to hear him explain his theory – that this was a model (perhaps a child's toy) of a larger structure, possibly ten feet in height . . . big enough to admit a man . . .

Yes! Impossible though it may seem, it is almost certain that early String-Age man actually lived in dwellings such as these! Cricklewood could have been the site of the very first village of little red pot huts!

"It looks like an old flower-pot to me!" muttered Bill Oddie as he stomped grumpily out of the tent. Tim and I looked at each other astounded. Why hadn't we seen it before – just as ancient man, looking up at the round red huts he lived in must suddenly have had the same impression – and invented flower-pots! Tim's eyes had begun to smoulder with the passion of a true archaeologist. His strong, bronzed arms were around me, and I knew then that (continued on p. 98)

Artist's reconstruction

CRICKLEWOOD MAN

DR. GRAEME GARDEN, working on fossil material found at the Cricklewood site, has come up with an astounding reconstruction of what is now recognised to be man's most ancient ancestor – the Missing Link – Cricklewood Man.

The face of Cricklewood man, unseen on this planet since the passing of the String-Age, has been painstakingly remodelled from fragments of the skull discovered by William Oddie, Dr Garden's assistant.

The British Museum, anxious to verify a discovery of this importance, have run tests on the material. They pronounced them genuine, and have put them on display to the public. Admission £1.40, Old Age Pensioners also on show.

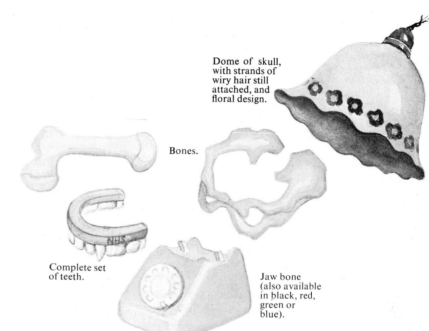

Dome of skull, with strands of wiry hair still attached, and floral design.

Bones.

Complete set of teeth.

Jaw bone (also available in black, red, green or blue).

FURTHER RESEARCH

and a great deal of inspired wild guessing has also enabled Dr Garden to have a bash at thinking up this detailed picture of our earliest ancestor in full. Note the protruding and crinkly forehead, big nose, and funny feet.

CRICKLEWOOD MAN SENSATION!

ROLL UP ROLL UP

TO THE

FABULOUS

BRITISH MUSEUM

INTRODUCING AT ENORMOUS EXPENSE

OUR NEW STAR ATTRACTION

CRICKLEWOOD MAN

RELIVE THE GLORIES OF THE STRING AGE

FULL SUPPORTING PLUS EXTRA

IT'S ALL HERE
ALL THE FUN OF THE MUSEUM
THE BALLYHOO
THE THRILLS
THE SILENCE

FABU

Egy

Rare

ADMISSI
£1·40 inc

AT THE BRIT

BRITISH MUSEUM

Dear Goodies,

Just a 'wee' note to say well done, a
warmly felt "ta very much" for your endeavours.
'Cricklewood Man' has been a great success, an
absolutely coining it here.

My word, we certainly fooled them. Beats Tuta
any day of the week. The trustees of the Museum
been discussing the possibility in the not too
future of taking the show on the road – however
must wait and see.

Thanks again – do drop in and see us someti

ion only £1.40)

atefully

Daily Mirror

PULL THE OTHER ONE, GOODIES – GRANDAD'S NO FROG!

THAT TROUBLESOME TRIO, THE GOODIES,
AT IT AGAIN! Now they're trying to tell us
Grandad had frog's legs! Even the
'ish Museum say so. Come off it!
be all right for France,
'ad of old boll-
kidding?

perts tend to
load of rubb
song voice,
theory does

THE Sun

STRING-AG
PHONEY NEW
FOOLED ME!

Or so says
shapely
Polish-born
archaeologist
Donna
Wannano.
This pert
Miss from
Krakow is
a doctor of
Archaeology
but she says
her aim is to
own her own
hair-dressing
salon and to
travel.
Meanwhile,
let's look at
her bosom!!

THE DAILY TELEGRAPH

CRICKLEWOOD MAN A HOAX!

Goodies accused. British Museum implicated in fraud.

DARWIN WAS RIGHT AFTER ALL!

In spite of suggestions by self-styled Archaeologists, the Goodies, it now seems that Charles Darwin's theory of the Origin of Species will remain intact. Recent claims by the Goodies of the discovery of ancient remains showing our ancestors with webbed feet and skinny legs, thus proving that our remote forefathers were descended, not from the apes, but from frogs, have been received with some reserve by Archaeologists who disagree. On the other hand, Archaeologists who don't disagree have tended to accept the idea.

The final straw seems to have been an illustration by Dr G. Garden showing Cricklewood man, with his well known facial features, in-cluding the so-called "telephone jaw", but showing him with web-feet and legs like a frog. When asked to comment on the Frog theory, Dr Garden replied "Hop it!"

"Are we descended from Frogs?" now seems to be the question of the day. Most leading archaeological experts tend to reply "What a load of rubbish!" in a sing song voice. However, the theory does have its supporter.

"I find it perfectly acceptable to believe that we were descended from frogs!" exclaimed noted Archaeologist Sir Andrew 'Toadface' Robinson.

On the other hand, Professor Gary "Gibbonfeatures" Potter claims that if we're not descended from the apes, we're not worth the paper we're printed on. Well that's his opinion and he's welcome to it. That's what I say at any rate.

Now look, be honest, I couldn't care less, but it seems clear to me that the Goodies (who let's face it do anything for cash) and the British Museum have joined forces to perpetrate a (money-making) hoax, to fool the people into shelling out the ready to gawp at a load of old rubbish for purely financial gain. Man descended from frogs? Oh do leave off!

Surely the *real* String-Age man was not Fulham F.C. However, the theory does have its supporter.

"V
an

My w
skis.
you d
reason
gives
occasi
and a
point
Sudde
taken
them,
stood
huma
above
colour
an ins
corrob
Opera
across
contro
senses
arms
much
the for
saying.
Appley
's a

Nevertheless so much been owed by so many to three people. Regards, Winnie

D. Day '46

To the Goodies why didn't we being out'ie been famous boys now... wear Groucho, Chico, Harpo & Zeppo "it - ?"

Its all up to you now lads You are the Walrus cheers, John Paul George R... JUN...

I can teach you nothing Peace & Love M... R...

From one Goody to the others, Bless you! Pious VI

This visitors book belongs to THE....GOODIE...

NAME	ADDRESS
Martin Boorman	no fixed abode the Jungle, Amazon
Mohammad Ali	% The Mohammed Alijah School of Speech + Dram Louisville Ken. U.S.A.
Tom & Jerry	"Loonyville" N. York U.S.A.
Richard Nixon	% Happilands Home for Ex Presidents, Florida.
General Amin	(from tomorrow... The World...)
MAO TSE TUNG	14 ACACIA ROAD PEKING N.W.4
Danny LaRue	Mother Kelly's Doorstep
"Pan's People"	BBC TV CENTRE

EXHIBIT E

AUTO TEST
The Goodies Trandem

The basic design of the Goodies Trandem has remained unchanged since its invention. There seems no point in wasting time trying to improve it. Some people would call it a unique disaster; but it has a charm all of its own. There are those who swear by it, and on it or about it. So let's find out more . . .

The Goodies Trandem is a three-seater model that combines ugliness with discomfort – an unparalleled combination for the hard-up, simple-minded or suicidal. One model only.

The Trandem is perhaps the Goodies' most re-markable achievement in the field of transport. In fact it is their only achievement in the field of transport; except of course for their feet – which are nothing to write home about. The Goodies Trandem, on the other hand, is most certainly something to write home about. Our testers – at present recovering in Cricklewood Infirmary – write home about it nearly every day. Their descriptions range from '****ing amazing!' to 'that God-forsaken old junk heap'. The truth probably lies somewhere beneath the two, but one thing is certain – the Trandem is unique. Quite simply, it has no serious competitors (although there are a few very silly ones). Both its nearest rivals – the German Volksdreical and the Japanese Triniped – have recently been declared illegal, which leaves the International Market wide open for the Goodies Trandem to make a killing – or at least cause serious injury. Unfortunately, distribution and supply leaves quite a lot to be desired. There is at present, only one trandem in existence, and although there is another one under consideration, there is bound to be a waiting period of between twelve years and eternity. What is more, the Goodies are only accepting a limited number of orders – namely, one. Prospective buyers should not be put off, however, as so far nobody has shown any interest whatsoever.

Performance

One of the chief boasts of the makers is that the Trandem uses up very little petrol; we found this claim utterly justified, except when we crashed into a service station and knocked over two pumps. The riders are normally driven by alcohol. They are, we discovered, quickly driven to alcohol. It was usually necessary to consume quite an intake before building up sufficient nerve to try and ride the Trandem. Make no mistake, this is a very powerful vehicle. The makers claim a top speed of over twenty miles an hour, but whilst this is certainly theoretically possible, our testers found that at anything over fifteen mph their legs were revolving at such a rate that they flew off, and

caused quite a hazard to passersby.

Ride and handling

The commonest complaint amongst our testers was they often felt 'Totally out of control', and this is something we feel the makers should look into. The Trandem does of course, have front-wheel drive, and in order to help suppress the natural temptation to use the handlebars (which are purely for balance) the makers provide safety belts for the second and third riders which securely fasten their hands behind their back.

Visibility is excellent all round, but this advantage is offset a little by the fact that most of our testers found it impossible to resist the powerful urge to close their eyes.

We would imagine that, once under way, riding the Trandem would be an exhilarating experience, but we're only guessing, as nobody managed to stay on for more than ten yards.

During that short distance we did consider that the Trandem was

rather a noisy ride. There's a distracting amount of panting, wheezing, cries of 'get me off this thing' etc. etc. We also found that there could be a disconcerting amount of wind noise; we would not recommend cycling after drinking Ginger Beer or eating baked beans.

Brakes

The brakes are almost totally ineffective, but we do not consider this to be a serious drawback, as they are very rarely necessary: half our testers never got moving, whilst the other half stopped with no difficulty, simply by falling off.

Fitting and furniture

The Trandem is a roomy vehicle and whilst it is built for three, one could easily get two people on the back saddle, though it would of course be extremely dangerous – though no more dangerous than normal. On the other hand, it can be ridden by two, or even one – or simply be left rusting away in the garden shed.

The seats are all adjustable, though it must surely be counted a fault that when the front saddle is at full height it is impossible to reach the handlebars. The basic design is

perhaps 'rugged' rather than 'luxurious', but there are innumerable 'extras' available. For example you can buy plush 'armchair' seats – not, in our opinion very practical as we found them very hard to balance on the saddles. Bucket seats are also available and we consider them of more use . . . especially for throwing up into.

The makers also provide an optional windscreen washer, but at present there is no optional windscreen. The effect is, however, very refreshing on hot days and waterproof diving goggles are available.

Several extra safety extras are also available including cushions for falling off onto; safety belts which anchor the riders to the nearest lamp post so they can't

move; and an oxy-acetylene cutter with which you can totally destroy the beastly vehicle.

In conclusion

Glancing through this report it might appear that our testers did not have a good word for the

Above: Luggage room is not generous – in fact it's soddin stingy. It can accommodate, however, a paper bag, a rabbit, or a small dwarf, though no dwarf we know enjoys it very much.

Below: This is the sort of power that gives the Goodies Trandem that really 'sporty' thrust.

Comparisons

MAXIMUM SPEED MPH

Concorde	**(£10,000,000)**	**1174**
Ford Cortina 2000E	(£2,262)	102
Hovercraft	(£25,000)	53
Goodies Trandem (any offers?)		**20**
Tortoise	(0·3p)	·01

OVERALL MPG

*Goodies Trandem	30·7
**Tortoise	25·6
Ford Cortina 2000E	24·1
Hovercraft	4·3
Concorde	0·02

*Per gallon of Newcastle Brown
**Per gallon of lettuce and potato peelings
N.B. Concorde will do 32·00 mpg on lettuce and potato peelings.

Performance

ACCELERATION

Speed mph	Time in secs	Bike* Speedo mph
0	14·2	5
5	30·6	5
10	65·9	5
15	432·0	5
20	6739·2	5

*Bike Speedo broken

Standing ¼ mile.
39 secs –10 mph

Standing standing
4 days – 0 mph

GEARING

1st person pedalling 5·4 mph per 100 rpm
2nd person pedalling 10·3 mph per 1000 rpm
3rd person pedalling 16·4 mph per 1000 rpm

Dimensions

STANDARD GARAGE. 16ft x 8ft 6ins

OVERALLS
OVERALL LENGTH 72"
OVERALL WIDTH 8'
18" 20" 21"
6"
6"
12" 6" 16" 19"
OVERALL HEIGHT 39"
12"
WHEELBASE 72"

Consumption

FUEL

Versatile – Goodies will run on almost anything, especially Newcastle Brown, Campari & Soda, Scotch & Ginger, Tequila Sunrise & Hot Chocolate – or any combination of these. (Mixture should not be too rich.)

OIL

Lubricating oil, Cooking Oil, Lard or Margarine. Chains and all moving parts – including knees – need oiling every 500 miles.

TEST CONDITIONS

Weather: pissing down
Wind: 3-95 mph ENW
Temperature: 'Brass Monkeys'
Humidity: 100 per cent
Surface: Wet asphalt, wet pavement, wet river bank & wet river
Test distance: 10 yards

Facia

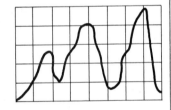

PENNANT → GO(DIES
HEADLIGHT
CIGARETTE LIGHTER & HEADLIGHT CONTROL.
BACK BRAKE
RADIO
DRIVING MIRROR
BELL
BROKEN SPEEDO
FRONT BRAKE
GLOVE COMPARTMENT
STEERING COLUMN.
INSTRUMENTS

Specification

FRONT-WHEEL DRIVE

ENGINE
Chains	2 usually broken
Pedals	6 Bent

WHEELS
Type	Round, slightly buckled
Spokes	Quite a lot, mostly wire some string
Tyres	Rubber, with elastoplast patches

STEERING
Type	Handlebars (front only practical)

CHASSIS AND BODY
Construction	Metal of some sort, finished in 'Blood Red' (real) and 'Rust' (also real)

Servicing

Not worth it

Below: Just a few of the luxury 'extras' available
1 *'Armchair' seats*
2 *'Bucket' seats*
3 *Heater (mains operated) carried by the 3rd rider – has the drawback that the vehicle can travel only as far as the flex allows.*
Above – right: Ultra obvious 'head-lamp' standard equipment. Great attention is paid to extra safety measures on the Trandem, largely because it's so bloody dangerous.

Trandem. Not so . . . they had several excellent words; amongst them: 's***t', '**ap', '*i**' and quite a few rather naughty ones too. However this is of course only personal opinion, and it is not beyond the bounds of credibility that someone somewhere might want to purchase a Goodies Trandem. Well, if you are remotely interested we are told that the Goodies are planning to bring out several other 'models' of the Trandem.

These include a one seater version (with only one set of pedals) and a 'Convertible' (which includes a 'conversion kit' of two more wheels, an engine, chassis, etc. etc.) *see illustration.*

Personally we feel that both these versions are somewhat contrary to the spirit of the original concept of the Trandem.

Some planned new versions'
Right: 'Single-seater' trandem

Above: 'Convertible' trandem

Below: 'Ocean-going luxury transatlantic' trandem

Above (right): '2 ton Centurian Military Service' trandem (as ordered by General Amin)

Anyway, suppose you still wanted to buy the standard model. Just suppose. How much will it cost you? The Goodies themselves have stated that they consider the vehicle to be 'Price-less'. Which is fair enough. So if you want it, you don't have to pay anything at all. We, however, feel that this is rather unfair. After all, you will be lumbered with carting it away, and you'll also have to put up with people laughing at you if you try and ride it. We would therefore recommend that you bargain with the Goodies, and if they've got any sense they'll slip you a couple of quid to take it away. But then they can't possibly have any sense, or they wouldn't have built it in the first place.

Anyway if you do buy it don't be too upset. It would make an ideal present to give to three people you really dislike – like, half the Osmond Brothers or Mary, Mungo and Midge etc.

ADVERTISEMENT

EXHIBIT F

It's Time for Tim

Bill's a Pill

TOP SECRET FILE

Title: *The Political File*

Let's go for Graeme

THE TROPICAL FISH FANCIER'S AND AQUARIST'S ARGUS

THIS MONTH IN THE LAW COURTS
by our Law Reporter – "Spy."

The Goodies V Weidenfeld & Nicolson

Disappointingly, there have been few references so far, in this fascinating legal tussle, to Tropical Fish – particularly the more exotic varieties which are gaining such popularity these days. Yesterday, for example, as the trial got into its full swing, the Goodies were called upon to defend themselves against the charge of being "Irresponsible." Mr Brooke-Taylor, defending himself, made no mention of goldfish. As he unfolded the complicated but impressive facts in his favour, there were cries of "Hear hear!" and "Right on!" from the public, but no mention of guppies or shibunkins. Aquarists present began to sense that things were to worse, and sure enough they

did. The judge, in summarising a subtle point of law, missed a heaven-sent opportunity to comment on the prevalence of gill-rot in the delicate Four-Eyed Butterfly Fish, so popular with fanciers in Crawley and parts of Leicester. "Well!" exclaimed Mr Brooke-Taylor at one juncture, "if you consider us to be irresponsible, I can only refer you to 'EXHIBIT F' – a file summarising our dedication to active participation in politics and the democratic process."

Here Vanessa Redgrave sprang from her seat in the public gallery and delivered an impassioned address. She did not refer to Longspine Squirrelfish.

Official Application Form for Parliamentary Leadership

SO YOU THINK YOU SHOULD BE

Prime Minister

Surname (last name): _TIM_

Christian Name (first name): _BROOKE_

Names in between: _TAYLER TAYLOR_

Nickname: _NICK_

Age: (if over 21, put "over 21") _MATURE_

Height (approx): _6 FOOT_

Weight (approx): _83 27943 Kg_

Sex (approx): _APPROX_

To which political party do you belong, if any? _ANY_

Have you ever held office in a Cabinet? If so give details of your achievements whilst in power _NO_

Are there any other offences you would like to be taken into consideration? _NONE (APPROX)_

Which political figure of the past do you most admire?
a) Lloyd George
b) Disraeli
c) Machiavelli
d) Attila the Hun
e) Attila the Liberal ✓

Arrange the following list of attributes according to their importance in the make-up of a Prime Minister:
a) Blue eyes
b) Pragmatism
c) Economic know-how
d) All own teeth   _Shan't._
e) Double-barrelled name
f) Seat belts
g) Skill in debate
h) Clean fingernails
i) Extensive repertoire of comic songs

Note: Any candidate arrogant enough to assume he is doing all right so far may proceed to the next section

Who is your favourite British male vocalist?
SHIRLEY BASSEY

Television technique
If you were addressing the Nation on TV, what would y do with your hands?
a) Hold them clasped in front of you on the desk ✓
b) Wave them around in the air like a greasy foreigner
c) Pick your nose ✓
d) Fondle the microphone ✓

Word Association
What word do you normally associate with each of the following?
a) Economic _CRISIS_
b) Financial _DISASTER_
c) Political _SUICIDE_
d) Bribery and _LOCAL GOVERNMENT_
e) Immediate _RESIGNATION_

Spelling
Can you spell "chrysanthemum"?
a) Yes ✓
b) No

Honesty
Can you *really* spell chrysanthemum?
a) Yes
b) My answer to the previous question seems to have bee misinterpreted in certain quarters. At no time have I tried give the false impression that I actually *could* spell chryssanthermum, merely that I *might* be able to: – which you will agree is a far cry from etc. etc. ✓

Parliamentary debating technique
As Prime Minister, how would you address the Leader the Opposition?
a) The honourable member with a big bum
b) Mouldy old stink-pot ✓
c) Grandma
d) Your worship
e) Ferret-face
f) Sausage-nose
g) Grot-bag

Declaration
I hereby declare that the above answers are true to the best of my knowledge and ability ✓

love from _Tim_

This form must be sealed in an envelope and sent to: His Nibs, 10 Downing Street, London, Nr. Godalming

To arrive not later than lunchtime

10 DOWNING STREET   LONDON

Dear Mr. Brooke-Taylor,

The Prime Minister has asked me to acknowledge the receipt of your application to become Prime Minister. He has also asked me to tell you a lot of things I can't spell, in fact most of the words I've never heard of. However, he did make it clear that if you don't keep your something hands off his something job, you'll find yourself up some sort of creek without an oar. He also hinted that he might send the Minister of Power round to make you an offer that you couldn't refuse. That would be nice wouldn't it?

Yours faithfully, *Miss T. Morning*

<u>Sec to Prime Minister</u>

P.S. If you really want to become Prime Minister, you have to be elected as an M.P. first.

Dear Bill + Graeme,
I have gone out for an hour or so to become Prime Minister. Your dinner is in the oven.
Love
Tim

Dear Graeme,
Have gone out for an hour or so. Your dinner is in my stomach...
Love B.M.

Dear Computer —
Have gone out for an hour or so. Your programme is in the safe.
I love you!
Irene XX
PS — Hope your transistors are feeling better.

Minister for Power resigns as MP

"He duffed me up" claims Union leader. Bye-election to be held on August 10th.

by Daily Mail Reporter

JARVIS PINK, Minister for Power, and MP for Allstations South, gave the following statement to the Press this morning:

"Firstly, although I am resigning, I would like to make it clear that I was nowhere near the man at the time of his alleged 'duffing up'. Secondly, if I *was* anywhere near him I certainly didn't touch him. Thirdly, if I did touch him, it was just an affectionate pat on the back. Fourthly, if I did kick his teeth in and break both his legs, then it was an accident. Anyone can slip on a banana skin, causing their feet to fly into the air. Can I be blamed if a passer-by places his teeth in the way? The two broken legs are a complete mystery, although I may have fallen awkwardly a couple of times".

From his hospital bed, the victim is believed to have said: "Ah ka peek, ah goh o eeth".

Jarvis Pink on holiday with two friend[s]

Page 2 col 4: The man the PM used to 'Lean on'.

the new RedCross code

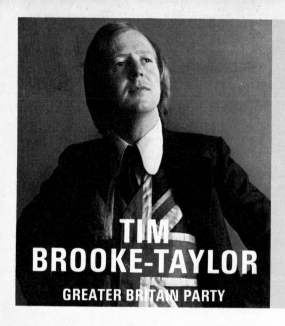

TIM BROOKE-TAYLOR
GREATER BRITAIN PARTY

Dear Electors,
I hope you are well I am.
Yesterday I went for a walk. It was drizzling. I want to be Prime Minister. Please vote for me
Thank you.
Tim Brooke-Taylor

GRAEME GARDEN LSP
(and if necessary Scottish Nationalist)

Dear Voter,

the world is now virtually controlled by loony scientists. Can this go on? With your help it can. Vote for me and you vote for your own loony scientist. Apart from that I would just like to say 'ping, pang, boodle, splat'.

Yours 'til it is resolved,

Graeme Garden

JUST HOW MAD AM I?

I like: Fishing, marzipan, standing on one leg with a finger in my ear, shouting 'I'm the letter P' – *and* 'Singalongamax records'

JUST HOW MAD ARE YOU?

Mad enough: to be interested in a 5 day cricket match that may have no result?
: to want to live in Britain?
: to believe in weather forecasts?
: to have read this far

If you say 'yes' to any of these, then you're mad
If not, go on . . .

Just one of my little experiments

BE MAD – VOTE FOR GRAEME

WHAT DO I STAND FOR?

The Queen
To have a pee
Liberty, fraternity and the other one
Women's rights and men's rights
Freedom of speech (within limits. No rude words)
The State, the Empire and the Essoldo
Better skools
Derby County
I believe : "Britain is still Great" and
"Flying Saucers Exist"

WHY TIM BROOKE-TAYLOR?

1 With me you will be represented by a knight –
   admittedly I'm not a knight yet, but if I was
   an MP it would be much more likely I would
   become one
2 (Sir) Tim Brooke-Taylor has never served on
   any local government bodies and is not an
   expert on anything. He can therefore be relied
   upon to approach everything with a blank mind
3 Why not ?

VOTE TIM BROOKE-TAYLOR
MAKE BRITAIN GREATOR

VOTE BILL ODDIE
(Little People's Revolutionary Party)

and *you* can get...

WOMEN

A body like this

A pension at 40

Free milk

The chance to do men's work

Green Shield stamps

MEN

Somebody like this

A pension at 30

Free beer

The chance to do *no* work

Lucky

DO YOU REALLY WANT...
To have all your money
taken away?   Your arms and legs chopped off?
To live in a communist/fascist* society?   *Delete where applicable
Nottingham Forest to win the Cup?

If your answer to these questions is "NO" or "NOT REALLY"
or "AS LONG AS IT DOESN'T HURT MUCH" – then vote for ME
or I'll smash your teeth in.

GIVE US A X

The Goodies prepare for their election campaign.

..Y JOSEPHINE

t five o'clock in the evening. I was riding my bike a. y business, which is more than can be said for sor as then that I beheld the most extraordinary sight . cleaning her front doorstep. She never cleans anythi n. The only time she cleans her teeth is when she mething. And it's not water she's drinking I can te oman she's a real . . .

with him, aving been ner during find I can ole in my my man r delight n. Your ave even adven- g than for my- of all years, asure for

m. I near ent. t my rly, is-

Graeme Garden appealing to the Liberals.

MIRROR COMMENT

Bill the Giant Killer

DAVID and Goliath, Jack and the Giant, Ronnie Corbet and the front doorstep, and now ... Bill Oddie and the Establishment.

The British working man has always liked his giants small. And so we, the Mirror, support Bill Oddie and his brave fight against Neo-scientific fascism.

Experiments on babies

WE CANNOT believe that Graeme Garden performs his experiments on babies and little puppy dogs.
WE CANNOT believe that Tim Brooke-Taylor has a private union-bashing army of 393 chartered accountants who train in a disused Chinese laundry just outside Rotherham.
WE WILL NOT believe these smears.
AND YET, there is no smoke without fire.

This is why the Mirror says: VOTE FOR BILL ODDIE.

Tim Brooke-Taylor making a bid for the Working Class vote.

Bill Oddie making an even bigger bid for the Working Class vote.

-Cat
MAGAZINE
SIASTS

e featuring
shionwear,
rwear and
ters etc.
copy of
e and lim-
so for £2
10. or Vol.2.
25 Pussy
No1 or No.2

for latest
Scandinavian
ar Brochure
re of Haute
ber garments
of Mayfair

P/Os to

DON.W1.

My wife and I...
This has many advantages ove...

Bill Oddie appealing to absolutely nobody

Mr...
above was the one rece...
coloured his judgement a little
an insurance salesman. Aren'
corroborative evidence from
Operative (Drunk) who was
across the sun and then I
controllable urge to take o
senses by a lady who was
arms in the air, screami
much credence should
the form of a statem
saying, "If this is
Appleyard died a
"It's a fair con...

DAILY EXPRESS
THE INDEPENDENT NEWSPAPER

OPINION

Some talk of Tim Brooke-Taylor

OF all the world's great heroes there's none that can compare . . . Yes there's none that can compare with a British hero. Drake, Nelson, Wellington, Churchill, Brooke-Taylor . . . the list is endless. But let's be fair. What has Europe to offer? Hitler, Mussolini, Stalin, Oddie, Garden . . .

We're not anti-foreign. We believe that an alien has every right to live in his own country. But we do not believe he has the right to steal our jobs and spank our women . . . that is a British right.

It's up to all of us to pull our fingers out of whatever we've got our fingers in. Strike a blow for a Greater Britain. Vote for Captain Brooke-Taylor, DSO and wooden leg.

Tim Brooke-Taylor explaining that recent defence cuts might have been too drastic.

THE FOLLOWING IS A STATEMENT BY ALAN HARGREAVES, Social risk operative. (Insured salesman)

new scientist

Comment

Our Docter in the 'House'

Who is it wot wrote, 'Scientists is illiterate'? Sir Isaac Newton, we think, or Ernie Wise done it. *But* here is Graeme Garden, a scientist which can string fourwords together. We know we know everything. Dr. Garden can tell everyone and rule the world for us.
DON'T be a complete Arts Graduate . . . vote Garden. You make it sense know.

Graeme Garden playing with a baby computer in his bid for the technocratic vote.

Uptadate Polls Ltd

Instructions to Pollsters

All sheets must be returned *correctly*, and must *accurately* reflect the voting intentions of your area.

All questions must be *voluntarily* answered by pollees

However, if by the end of the day you are still short of your quota you may use your discretion.

But: Absolutely *no* offensive weapons may be used, unless you are wearing gloves.

No visual marks should be left on Pollees.

(NB *Pollees* **not** *Police*)

Name: R. U. Bonkers
Occupation: Rodent suppressor
Sex: Not anymore
Age: See above

	YES	NO	DON'T KNOW
1. Which do you prefer:			
A. This delicious margarine?		✓	
or B. This rather tasteless butter?		✓	
2. Which does your pet prefer to eat:			
A. Stratford Johns?		✓	
B. Clement Freud?	✓		
or C. A top breeder?		✓	
3. Which is your favourite TV programme:			
A. Crossroads?	✓		
B. Crossroads?	✓		
C. Crossroads?	✓		
or D. Crossroads?		✓	
4. Which socio-economic group do you belong to:			
1. A+			✓
2. A/B			✓
3. C			✓
4. D			✓
or 5. Irish	✓		
5. I know it's a bore, but if you <u>had</u> to vote, who would you vote for?			
A. Graeme Garden			✓
B. Bill Oddie			✓
C. Tim Brooke-Taylor			✓
or D. Don't know	✓		

Shock Poll Figures

tandard Reporter

here was a shock to-day r the three major candi-ates in the Allstations outh bye-election.

According to an Uptadate Poll, aken on Monday, the 'Don't Knows' have shot into a one hundred percent lead. Tim Brooke-Taylor, electioneering to-day in the Goat and Compasses Turkish Baths in Heath Street, said "Take your hand off my knee". He then went on to say: "Personally I have great faith in the British electorate and will you stop that at once". Graeme Garden, on his tour of the North, brought a little cheer to Preston's city centre by marching up and down, and singing 'If I ruled the world'. He went on to say: "Aaaaagh!" as he fell down an uncovered manhole. Bill Oddie got a round of applause from shoppers in Allstations Market Place this morning when he produced a rabbit and flags of all the nations out of a policeman's helmet. He also got a £10 fine and a warning when he produced a brick out of the same police-man's pocket.

Greater Britain Party

**Headquarters:
Mary Whitehouse House
Cricklewood**

Dear Bill,

Whatever 'the other one' may have thought, you and I have always stuck together. I have a suggestion. If one of us were to retire from the contest (I was thinking of you actually) there would be no chance of Mr Smartypants, 'Giglamps' Garden winning. You know what he's like now, making us wash our hands before we eat a bag of crisps! Just think, Comrade, what he'd be like if he became prime minister! Compulsory baths!

Your brother in arms,

Tim

PS Play your cards right and I'll make you minister of sport (free cup final tickets, a chance to meet Olga Korbut etc.)

reater Britain Party

**Headquarters:
Mary Whitehouse House
Cricklewood**

Dear Graeme,

Whatever 'the other one' might have thought, you and I have always stuck together. You are one of the talented few and, believe me, no one appreciates those talents more than I do.

What a shame if you became an M.P. and had to drop all those experiments! What a mess! An M.P. has to do a lot of boring things. That sort of work is best left to people like, well, me. With your votes I can beat that money-grubbing, Commie dwarf. What do you say?

Your admiring friend.

Tim

PS You can have my share of the holiday money.

Dear Tim

Get stuffed!

Love

Bill

Oscar Wilde strikes again!
T.B.T

Dear Tim

You can't blame me. I've already taken your share of the holiday money,

Received with thanks — £1-25½p

Graeme Garden

My dear diary,
This is the day
With me luck.
Good nion: my stars
say "Good day for
those seeking new
positions"!

"Cant beat, cant beat, the
Parliamentary Rork.
Cant cheat, cant cheat, the
Electoral Roll
my feet are sweet ..."
Hey, my stars say "Good
day for those seeking new
positions"!

Dear diary
My computer has
been behaving strangely -
probably resents my being
out so much. My stars
say 'good day for shopping'
So I'm going to tell the
Police about Tim & Bill

	Place your 'x' here
ODDIE W.E. Little People	
GARDEN Dr. D.G. L.S.P.	Do not give this ballot paper away sweeties, or it will become spoilt. Teehee
BROOKE-TAYLOR T.J. Greater Britain	
OTHER A.N.	**SPOILT**

Bye-election Shock

COMPUTER WINS BY WIDE MARGIN

Mr. A N Other surprised all parties to-day by getting one hundred percent of the vote in the Allstations South bye-election. Mr. Other, in a surprise victory print-out to his supporters, declared that his successful campaign would not have been possible without a thriving party machine. The machine is believed to have been an IBM 42L

Disappointing

A spokesman for Upta-date Polls Ltd. said, this morning: "We have never, at any time, claimed one hundred per-cent accuracy for our polls. The fact that on this occasion they were one hundred percent in-accurate, although a little disappointing, should not be exaggera-ted. They were, after all, still within the margin of error that we allow ourselves". The spokes-man then added: "This small setback should not be allowed to erode the public's confidence in opinion polls". He then retired behind a screen and shot himself.

32
34 DEAR GOODIES
36 HOPE YOU DONT MIND STOP
38 HAVE RUN AWAY
40 TO BECOME PRIME MINISTER STOP
42 YOUR DINNER IS IN THE OVEN STOP
44 LOVE FROM GRAEME'S COMPUTER
ALIAS A N OTHER

THE GOODIES BOOK OF ART

The Goodies Digest Association

Office of the Vice President
(Sales Division)
The Goodies Digest Association,
Not known at this address,
Cricklewood,
London PR1 DE

XHIBIT G

Dear Subscriber,

IMPORTANT NEWS!

Please find **enclosed** a copy of the magnificent new "GOODIES BOOK OF ART",
yours to enjoy COMPLETELY FREE for a trial period of two hours, after
which, if you haven't coughed up, we'll be round to your placé with the
frighteners. <u>THIS IS AN OFFER YOU CAN'T MISS!</u>

This book will be sold in the shops for £5, but by buying it now you can
actually make a profit of £1.50 for us by paying the incredible special
price of only £6.50; and get a valuable FREE GIFT into the bargain.
YES! Every subscriber who buys "THE GOODIES BOOK OF ART" before reaching
the end of this letter is entitled to a stupendous FREE Renaissance-style
pair of lovely, elegant, matching bicycle clips! They're yours - even if
you don't buy the book.

ITS SO SIMPLE! ALL YOU HAVE TO DO IS CUT OUT THE REPLY COUPON STATING YES
OR NO AND SEND IT TO US. SEND NO MONEY NOW! WE'LL MAKE SURE YOU SEND US
LOTS LATER.

A chance to see, in the comfort of your home, such masterpieces as this

Man being attacked by a fig leaf

YES!

Please rush me a copy of
THE GOODIES BOOK OF ART,
or my children would not
forgive me. We owe it to
the kids to see they are
given the right values.
Your book will certainly
give things we never had
before. God bless you!

NO!

Don't send me the book as
I am a complete idiot and
I don't have the sense to
know a good thing when I
see it. Really I couldn't
care less if people think
I am a dull lttle nobody,
and pretty stupid as well
as that

PAINTING
WHAT'S IT ALL ABOUT?

Old Masters – Scaling the Heights of Technical Accomplishment.
The Art of Painting is perhaps the most dazzling of Man's spiritual endeavours towards the creation of something which transcends the mere physical boundaries of this world and projects some cosmic relevance, and has of course been going on for years. Indeed the origins of painting are lost in the mists of antiquity, but nevertheless, enough masterpieces have been handed down over the years to provide a lifetime of study for the scholar, or joy for the connoisseur, and you've got to admit th most of them are pretty easy on the eye. And it soon become clear that the Old Masters of the Art scaled amazing heights o Technical Accomplishment.

Inspiration – or Tricks of the Trade?
However, it must be said that the technique of painting is base on a few simple rules, and a brief study of the history of Art wi serve to show the reader how true this is.

It's Easel-y Done!
Not so much a mistake this time – just sheer bad luck.
The bespangled girl in the picture is one Mary Tudor and it is just too bad for Antonio Moro that Mary blinked and moved her head just at the very instant her portrait was being painted.

There's a Lot of It about, Grandma!
Johannes van Eyck, the noted Flemish painter, ran into problems with h picture of "The Betrothal of Arnolfini" which he could easily have avoided b just following the basic rules. Carelessness in lining up the canvas has resulte in the picture being on the slant – and he's even cut off one of his subject heads! A little practice should be all that's necessary for the novice to achieve good result.

Mona by Flashlight.
But in the Art world nothing stands still for long. New innovations come, and old innovations go, and of course it wasn't long before good old Leonardo da Vinci was muscling in on the act. His most notable contribution to painting was the invention of the Flash Picture. Leonardo had a device fitted to his palette which consisted of a very bright magnesium flare which could be let off to illuminate the subject, which could then be painted very quickly by the artist. This meant that indoor subjects, previously too dark to paint, could now be captured by the use of Leonardo's flash technique. The only drawback, as the old man himself discovered, was that portrait subjects were sometimes dazzled so that a relaxed and natural expression was not easy to achieve. Sadly, Leonardo abandoned his experiments, and devoted his energies to inventing the telephone. (Incidentally, Leonardo da Vinci did successfully invent and build the first telephone – but of course it was useless until years later Alexander Graham Bell invented the other one. Sadly, when Bell eventually called him, Leonardo had already been dead for over three centuries, and was unable to come to the phone. All this is fascinating you will agree but has little to do with painting.)

It Moves – It Moves!!

Painting was growing up. And it is to Botticelli we owe thanks for the development of what he called "Motion Paintings" – pictures that for the first time actually moved, and which were later, of course, to be completely forgotten. Unfortunately, all that remain of this great artist's work are a few frames like the three illustrated above from his famous "Venus" sequence. It must be admitted that his Motion Paintings were not an unqualified success. He achieved the effect of movement by painting a series of canvasses in which the positions of his subjects were slightly altered. These canvasses were then hung, in correct sequence, down the side of the leaning tower of Pisa. To experience the illusion, the observer would then have to jump off the top of the tower, looking at the pictures as he fell, but only opening his eyes momentarily as he passed each one, thus seeing a sequence of images giving the impression of continuous motion. It was not as popular an attraction as Botticelli had hoped. Nevertheless, this fine painter and supreme showman will always be remembered, for he, like Walt Disney, did not invent the telephone.

And Brueghel came too.

It is said that another painter who experimented with moving pictures was none other than Pieter Brueghel (and if you're having any trouble with that name, it's pronounced Peter.). His masterpiece "A Country Wedding" was justly famous, and ran for twenty minutes with a special sound accompaniment by Cipriano de Rore. Alas, only a single frame survives, showing the peasants gathered round the table just before the celebrated custard pie sequence.

Strength to Strength.

And so painting went from strength to strength. But the old order changeth, and new stars began to appear in the firmament. At the end of the 19th century the Art world was shocked by the advent of the Impressionists – Manet, Sisley, Degas, and of course Renoir, seen here doing his notorious Impression of Queen Victoria. When asked why he did it, he invariably replied "I'm only in it for the Monet". He was best known as a painter.

The Post-Impressionists.

Not surprisingly, the Impressionists were soon followed by the Post-Impressionists – most notably Paul Cezanne – shown, in this portrait by Van Gogh, doing an impression of a post.

Photography.

At last, Photography eventuated. The new art form was to supersede painting. Now it was a simple matter to capture the subject in detail, realistically and with absolute precision, as we can see from this photograph of a painting by Paul Klee.

HOW WE REVIVED A FADING MASTERPIECE

by Graeme Garden

Whistler's Mother

*The Art of Restoring Paintings demands great patience and ski[ll]
as we found out only the other week when we had a bash at [it]
ourselves.*

*Of course we'd read a bit about it, so we knew what we were doing.
Anyway, when the trustees of the Louvre in Paris found out wh[o]
we were, they were only too pleased to give us a picture to try o[ur]
luck with. As it happens, they decided that Whistler's famou[s]
picture of his mother, better known as "Whistler's Mother", w[as]
a bit grubby, so they handed it over, and away we went, proud[ly]
carrying this wonderful masterpiece.*

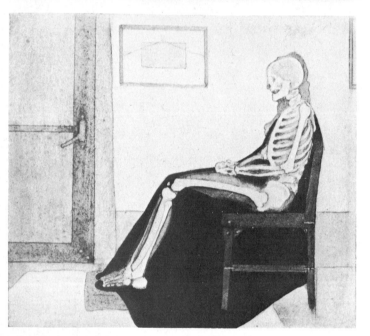

Whistler's Mother X-rayed.

*Well, as anyone knows, the first thing to be done before restoring [a]
painting is to have it X-rayed, so one rainy Wednesday morning, off we [went]
Tim to the Royal Expensive Hospital's X-Ray department where he m[et]
Professor Reichenbaum who specialises in X-Rays. This is the picture [he]
took, and, according to the professor, apart from a little osteo-arthri[tis]
in the left knee, the old lady looks in pretty fair shape.*

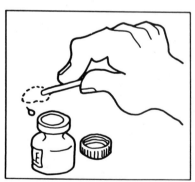

Stripping Mrs Whistler.

*Believe you me, it was with some trepidation that we began the job o[f]
cleaning it up! Very gently we sponged the surface with special cleanin[g]
fluid on a cotton swab – and held our breaths as the layers of accumulate[d]
dirt were removed. Suddenly Bill gave a little cry! The vague outline of [a]
leg had appeared! Tim rubbed even harder, and sure enough, there wa[s]
the unmistakable shape of a female leg peeping out from Madam[e]
Whistler's skirt! Was there more to be revealed we wondered . . .? W[e]
were itching to know . . .!*

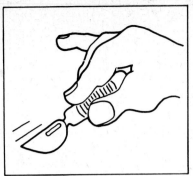

Scratch It.
According to the Blue Peter Book of Picture Restoration, *the next step is to scrape away the old layers of dirt and caked varnish which have built up over the years. This we did very gently with a sharp scalpel. Imagine our delight on discovering that La Whistler was apparently riding on a Stag – somewhat reminiscent of the "Monarch of the Glen" by Landscape. Or perhaps this was only an illusion – either way, we were determined that the old lady should yield her secrets!*

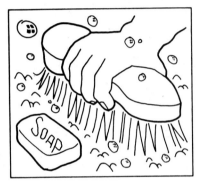

Old Scrubber.
Our preliminary work having promised so much, we set to with a vengeance to start the cleaning proper. Well, you can't beat a good old scrubbing brush and soapy water in my book – and since this is my book, that's exactly what we tried next. Well! I just don't know what you thought you were up to Mr James Abbott McNeill Whistler – but if you think a picture of King Henry VIII with a pair of horns is a suitable companion for your own mother, then all I can say is "do leave off!" However, I must say, we could hardly wait to see what would be revealed when the next layer of paint had been carefully stripped away . . .

A Fishy Business.
The old soap and scrubbing brush having proved too slow, Bill suggested we try smashing away at the paint with a hammer and chisel. As it turned out, this turned out to be quite a success. The horny king had apparently been painted on top of a still life featuring a bunch of grapes and a few cod, the sort of arrangement much favoured by several of the later Dutch school, but unlikely to find itself adorning the lounge walls of yours truly, but then that's only my opinion.

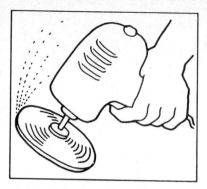

Blakandekkablakandekkablakandekkablakandekka . . .

Regretfully, we abandoned the hammer and chisel method of pictu[re] restoration after Tim had inadvertantly hit his thumb, and called o[ut] "Oh **** and ******* ****!!!" quite loudly. From now on, we were [to] treat the fragile old canvas with more care, consideration, and [an] electric sander. "Squeeeeeeeeeeeeeeeeeee!!!!!!" went the electric sande[r] "**** off!!" went Tim, nursing his thumb. But before long, the miraculo[us] device had peeled off yet another layer, to reveal that beneath all the oth[er] rubbish was a Renaissance portrait of Job, depicted standing in front [of] King Henry VIII with horns on, with Dame Whistler up his left nost[ril.]

Cleaner than Clean.

It was at this precise moment that Bill, keen student that he is of T[V] commercials, pointed out that if we wanted this canvas "cleaner th[an] clean", then we could do no better than try a spot of 'Thatsit!' bleach[—] none whiter. It was the work of but a moment to scour the picture wi[th] 'Thatsit' – and what can compare with the satisfaction of beholdi[ng] "Whistler's Mother" a pure, flat, shining WHITE!

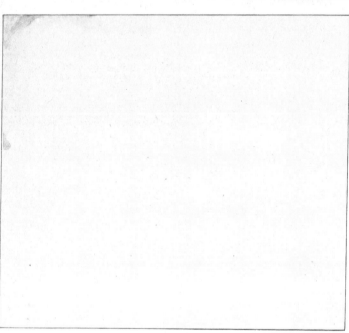

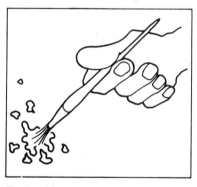

Re-touching.

After the friendly, but rather pointed phone call from the Louvre aski[ng] when they were getting their masterpiece back, we decided it was ti[me] for a little re-touching. Bill dashed off a quick Whistler's Mum, and [we] sent it off to them. So far we haven't heard from them, but I expe[ct] they'll get around to thanking us sometime soon. Mighty good fun th[is] picture restoring lark, eh gang?!

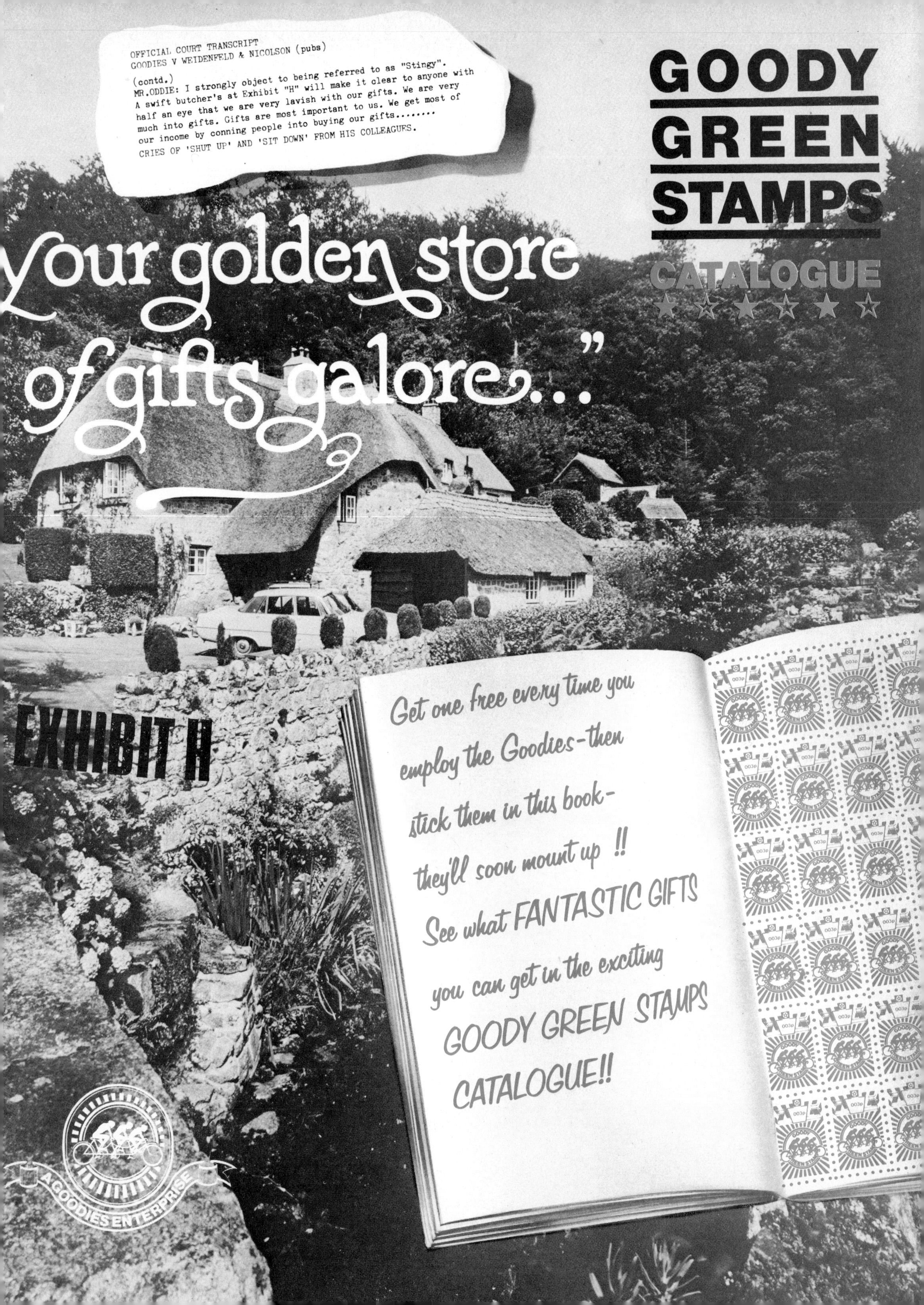

OFFICIAL COURT TRANSCRIPT
GOODIES V WEIDENFELD & NICOLSON (pubs)
(contd.)
MR.ODDIE: I strongly object to being referred to as "Stingy". A swift butcher's at Exhibit "H" will make it clear to anyone with half an eye that we are very lavish with our gifts. We are very much into gifts. Gifts are most important to us. We get most of our income by conning people into buying our gifts........
CRIES OF 'SHUT UP' AND 'SIT DOWN' FROM HIS COLLEAGUES.
GOODY GREEN STAMPS
CATALOGUE
"your golden store of gifts galore..."
EXHIBIT H
Get one free every time you employ the Goodies-then stick them in this book- they'll soon mount up !!
See what FANTASTIC GIFTS you can get in the exciting GOODY GREEN STAMPS CATALOGUE!!
A GOODIES ENTERPRISE

GOODY GREEN STAMPS!

1. **SET** of white kitchen stools. Not as nice as they look. 180

2. **MODERN** chess pieces. 45

3. **LOVELY** Italian floor tiles. You too can accidentally put them on the wall. 983½

4. **DEAD** Koala bear. Cute and unhygienic. 13

5. **STRING** of dried sheep's eyes. (An old country charm, guaranteed to fill the home with good luck and flies). 27

6. **SMALL** shirt, suitable for a boy or short adult. 27

7. **"MONTEZUMA":** exciting new dimension in cooking – combined oven/hob/grill/radio/cassette player/camera. Now you can take a picture of yourself dancing while you cook, if you want to. 983½

8. **"SPICY SWEDISH MAID!"** Life size, natural colour, (feels just like the real thing), absolutely realistic inflatable model of a spice rack. 254¾

9. **WHOOPEE** soap! Just place this ordinary seeming cake of soap on a chair, then when your unsuspecting guest sits down on it – whoopee! – their face goes black. 85

10. **USEFUL** solid hard-wood, teak-finished loaf of bread. Absolutely impossible to eat. 983½

11. **VISTA-VU** glue-on imitation window. Simply moisten the back and stick on wall, then watch it peel off. 180

12. **COFFEE** set including egg. 180

13. **LITTLE** black square thing lying on the floor with '13' on it. 13

14. **KITCHEN** gnome. 983½

15. **PERFECTLY** ordinary kettle. (Fuse and detonators extra). 180

GORGEOUS GIFTS!!!!

16. GREEN thing to hang from the ceiling. Will provoke hours of entertaining conversation: e.g. "Please take that green thing off the ceiling." (Comes complete with red thing.) **11**

17. HUGE bunch of flowers, which will eventually die. **12**

18. UNCLE Ben. You're welcome to him. **0**

19. REALLY nice shirt **1**

20. INCREDIBLY realistic working model of two nubile young French people at it like knives. Very naughty! **8¾**

21. THOROUGHLY dependable floor **3**

22. ITCHING chair! An absolute wow! Sit them down in this chair, then wait for them to start itching!! Sooner or later, they *just* might, though it's unlikely. **95¼**

23. "HAMILTON" wig, in choice of colours: blond, brunette, strawberry, blackcurrant, salt 'n' vinegar, camembert, or just plain – also in various sizes: small, medium, large, extra-large, enormously large, or hamilton. **1–983½**

24. "TELEPHONE" ornamental table-lighter. Looks just like a telephone, and what's more, you can't light cigarettes with it either! **180**

25. Left-overs. **13**

TIMBO MUSIC LTD

THE Tim Brooke-Taylor SONG BOOK

EXHIBIT I

INTRODUCTION
by
Tim Brooke-Taylor

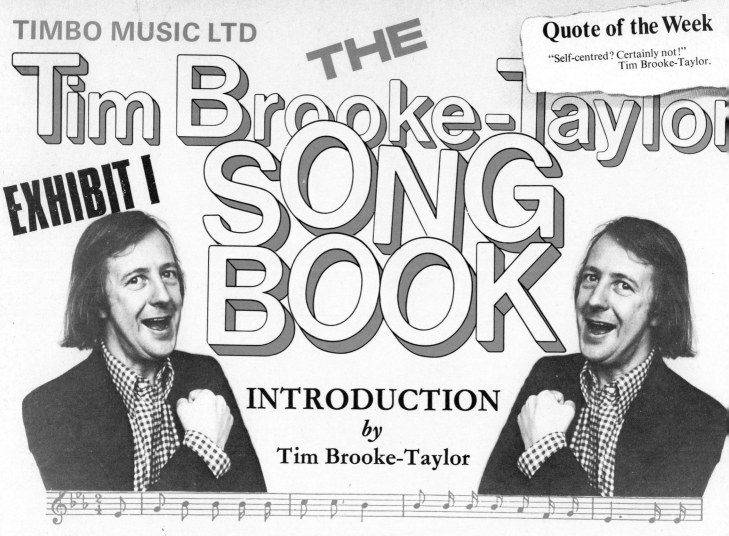

Down the years I have written many songs, most of them of a very personal nature. Up to now, I have very rarely sung any of them in public, nor even published the lyrics (remarkable though they are). However, lately, I have been inundated with letters from people telling me how much they would enjoy being able to sing about me, and, well, who am I to deny them the pleasure? After all, I may as well admit, *I* rather enjoy it too. And so here is the "Tim Brooke-Taylor Song Book" – I do hope you won't be disappointed. I'm sure we'll all derive hours of pleasure from the songs – they can be sung anywhere, as loud as you like, and as often as possible. I must admit I think they're just great – Hope you agree. Good singing . . .

First a few we can all join in . . .

(To the tune of "Rule Britannia")
Tim Brooke Taylor Brooke Taylor we love you
We love little Tim Brooke Taylor Yes we do.

(To the tune of "She'll be coming Round the Mountains")
She'll be riding Tim Brooke Taylor when she comes
She'll be riding Tim Brooke Taylor when she comes
She'll be riding Tim Brooke Taylor Riding Tim Brooke Taylor
She'll be riding Tim Brooke Taylor when she comes.
Singing Tim Brooke Taylor Yippeeyay
Singing Tim Brooke Taylor Yippeeyay etc. etc.
She'll be kissing Tim Brooke Taylor . . .
She'll be loving Tim Brooke Taylor . . .
She'll be worshipping Tim Brooke Taylor . . . and so on . . .

(To the tune of "The British Grenadiers")
Some sing of Tim Brooke Taylor, and Some of T.B.T.
Of Timothy Brooke Taylor, And such great names as "me"
We all love Tim Brooke Taylor, So let's all sing along.
With a Tim Tim Tim Tim Tim Tim—
That's the Tim Brooke Taylor song.

(To the tune of "I got Rhythm")
Tim Brooke Taylor
Tim Brooke Taylor
Tim Brooke Taylor
Who could ask for anything more?

(To the tune of "Camptown Races")
Oh Tim Brooke Taylor sings this song Timbo Timbo
Tim Brooke Taylor's never wrong. Timbo Timbo Day.

All compositions on this page by Tim Brooke-Taylor
© Timbo Music Ltd.

THE TIM BROOKE-TAYLOR SONG BOOK

TIMBO MUSIC LTD

And some with an International Flavour!

(To the tune of "When Irish Eyes are Smiling")
When I'm with Tim Brooke Taylor
Sure the world is bright and gay
Oh Darling Tim Brooke Taylor
He could charm the I.R.A.
He wears an Irish sweater
And he loves an Irish Stew
And his hair is soft and yellow . . .
And that's an "Irish" too!

(To the tune of "Oklahoma")
Tiiiiiiiiiiiiiiiiiiiiiiim Brooke Taylor
He's the butchest cowboy in the west.
He totes a gun, and he's lots of fun.
Yes Tim Brooke Taylor is the best.
Tiiiiiiiiiiiiiiiiiiiiiiim Brooke Taylor
Tiiiiiiiiiiiiiiiiiiiiiiiiiiiim Brooke Taylor
Three cheers for Tim Brooke Taylor
Tim Brooke Taylor—Hooray! hooray . . . (hooray)

(To the tune of "Bridges of Paris")
How would you like to be
Lovely as T.B.T.?

(To the tune of "Chicago")
Brooke Taylor Brooke Taylor That toddlin' Tim
Brooke Taylor Brooke Taylor He's ever so slim
When you're in Chicago They all like to holler
"Brooke Taylor! Brooke Taylor!" etc. etc.

(To the tune of "Arreverderci Roma")
We love you Tim Brooke Taylor
Italians all sing.

And some Music-Hall Favorites!

(To the tune of "Leaning on the Lamp-post")
I'm leaning on the lamp-post
At the corner of the street
For a certain Tim Brooke Taylor to come by . . .
Oh me oh my
Oh I hope that Tim Brooke Taylor comes by.

(To the tune of "My Old Man Said follow the van")
My old man said follow the van
And bring Tim Brooke Taylor on the way.

(To the tune of "My Old Man's a dustman")
Oh I like Tim Brooke Taylor
Brooke Taylor is a gent
Yes I like a Tim Brooke Taylor
Though people say he's bent.
We all know Tim Brooke Taylor
Likes dressing up in drag.
But if you say That Timbo's gay
He'll hit you with his bag! Whoops . . .

And even Rock and Roll – oh yes!

(To the tune of "See you later Alligator")
See you later Tim Brooke Taylor . . .

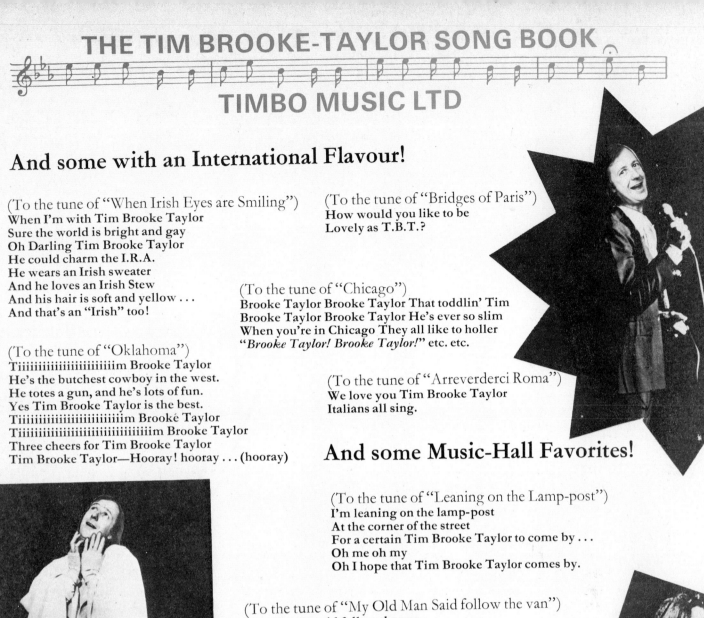

I Left My Heart
IN TIM BROOKE-TAYLOR
TONY BENNETT

Simon and Garfunkel
Bridge Over Tim Brooke Taylor

AND HAVE YOU HEARD
THESE *BEST-SELLING* LP's?

MRS MARY WHITEARSE

President of Keep Filth off Cliff Richard Campaign
and
Personal Adviser to BBC Light Entertainment Dept.

Dear Goodies,

(I hope you will take the word 'Dear' in the spirit that it is meant,
and nothing else.....)

I have a complaint about the vast numbers of smutty magazines appearing
on our bookstalls, all dedicated to the glorification of s*x. It seems
to me that one cannot buy a n*wsp*p*r these days without being faced
w*th a display of n*ked p*ople.

For years I and millions of other nice middle-aged ladies have been
forced to look at titillating pictures of young women, meant presumably
to excite young men.
Now, would you believe it, there are magazines for young women showing
lascivious pictures of young men! Well, it's <u>not</u> right is it?

So what are you going to do about it?

Yours (but only platonically)

Mary Whitearse

Mrs M.W.

EXHIBIT J

THE GOODIES
No Fixed Abode, Nr. Cricklewood, London

Dear Mrs W,
(Take it how you like, darling!)
Point taken, me love. It's all very well for
us young swingers, isn't ? But what about a little
titillation for you <u>oldsters</u> eh ? Fair enough, my
lovely - after all you're not past it yet, are you ?
- or perhaps I should ask Mr Whitearse eh ? eh ?
Anyway, no sooner mentioned than "voila" - enclosed
is a free copy for your approval, but let us have
it back when you're done drooling!
Right on gal,
Love (and all that),

Bill Oddie

(for THE GOODIES)

OLD MAID ONLY

Entertainment for Middle-aged Ladies
Volume 1 Number 1 75 pence
France 75 francs, Canada & USA $75
Australia & New Zealand–not available
NOT TO BE SOLD TO PERSONS
UNDER SIXTY YEARS OF AGE

EROTIC DANCES
(A NEW SLIGHTLY SAUCY
WAY TO DO
THE DINKY TWO STEP)

TIMONA TESTING THE TEA
MAKING OF THE GENTRY

GIGOLOS FOR SALE!
(THE TRAFFIC IN
RETIRED COLONELS EXPOSED)

EXCLUSIVE INTERVIEW
WITH LIBERACE–THE MAN
BEHIND THE MAN

PLUS
THE WORLD'S SAUCIEST MEN

PUBLISHED BY
THE GOODIES

FREE INSIDE
SAUCY 1976
CALENDAR

Question It's long, it's brown, and it's deeply satisfying. What is it Anona?

Answer Mm. Sorry, I'll tell you when I've finished my **MILK STOUT**

And, like love, MILK STOUT can be enjoyed a hundred different ways & then some! Try these for a start –

STOUT ON THE ROCKS – with half a brick in it.

STOUT SLING – just chuck it away.

STOUT SUNRISE – with pepper, corn, prunes & Senapods – gets you going in the morning.

STOUT SOUR – leave it standing for 3 weeks.

MILK STOUT *says it all*

Contents

Old Maid Only Vol 1 No 1.

Editorial

Well it was a bit of an effort – but we made it! Words that seem particularly appropriate in the context of this magazine.

Still – here – at last – is the second edition of OLD MAID ONLY. I'm sure you all agree it is a breakthrough in "entertainment" for the more mature lady. We've tried to be tasteful but at the same time . . . We've tried to make it pretty saucy! Perhaps we've tried too hard. 64 pages of this issue are at present under consideration by the Director of Public Prosecutions. This

means that your copy might seem a little lightweight; but we hope to make up for this when – and if – we publish Number 2. Rest assured, we are planning to – and it'll be saucier yet – but we're afraid there's bound to be a delay in publication, what with money problems, strikes, measles & total lack of interest – and of course by the time it does come out, many of you will probably be dead. Still, you've got number one to be getting on with and it is packed with *Cont. on page 14.*

The publisher regrets that pages 3 to 42, 44 to 55, 57 to 61, 63 to 73
and the back cover have had to be omitted from this issue.

ART DIRECTION: *Anthony Cohen* **DESIGNED BY:** *Dennis Hawkins, Philip Bryden, Arnaldo Putzu, Mike Wade, Geoff Halpin, Michael Lloyd, Arthur Ranson, Victoria Franklin, Derek Burton, John Leach, Mike Spiller, Phil Dobson, Jonathan Seddon-Harvey, Christine Copsey, Simon Bell.*	**PHOTO ACKNOWLEDGMENTS:** *BBC Pictorial Publicity, Don Smith (Radio Times), Spectrum Colour, Mansell Collection, Camera Press, Marshall Cavendish, British Film Institute, Transworld Feature Syndicate Incorporated, Coloursport.*
	With special thanks to: *Schreiber International, Graham 'Vicar' Capper, John Pink, Mrs Tole*
PHOTOGRAPHY BY: *Derek Burton, Geoff Goode.*	**Legal Advice:** *Ziman and Aarons*

Any time

Madam, My husband has recently taken to making love before, and whenever, the fancy takes him, no matter what I happen to be doing at the time.

I.V.
London.
P.S. Please excuse shaky handwriting.

On the buses

Madam, I'm sure many of your readers would be interested to hear of the remarkably pleasurable series of incidents that you have experienced whilst travelling on London Transport Buses lately.

Two weeks ago I was off to collect my pension during the rush hour on a no. 65 (Peckham to Bow St. every 15 minutes) and was forced to stand, there being no empty seats (which doesn't often happen actually) and thinking to myself how nice it would be if a young man were to offer me his seat (the seats are, by the way, extremely nicely upholstered and very comfortable). No sooner had the thought crossed my mind when, imagine my surprise – the man in front of me leapt to his feet and, imagine my surprise – when he turned out to be Steve McQueen.

As I sat down I couldn't help noticing the way his hand accidentally caressed the ivory duck handle of my umbrella. Well . . . to cut a long story short, in no time at all, we were making mad passionate conversation; and so engrossed were we that I went two stops past Balls Pond Road, where I normally get off.

Well, I thought, that was a bit of luck but I don't suppose it'll ever happen again. However the very next day I was travelling to the cemetery on a no. 12 (Chorley to Wandsworth, every 10 mins. except Sundays). and imagine my surprise – when I find myself sitting next to Marlon Brando – and yes! – the same thing happened. Since then I have had a similar experience on a no. 7 (Hampstead to Neasden). no. 34a, no. 62a and 6 and the relief service to White City, involving Tom Jones, Sacha Distel, Paul Newman, Hughie Green and Ronnie Corbett (twice).

I don't know if the particularly sensual movement of London Transport buses has anything to do with it, but I do know I shall never travel by tube or taxi again – and I have sold my motorbike.

I am a perfectly average elderly lady, not remarkably pretty and absolutely normal in all respects – and I see no reason why any or all of your readers should not have equally enjoyable experiences.

George Molebind
Public Relations Officer
(London Transport Buses Ltd)

Correspondence Coarse

An opportunity for you to put down on paper all those naughty words you pretend to have forgotten the meaning of – or perhaps you never knew them in the first place – or even if you did know them, you'd never actually say them. But you don't half like seeing them in print don't you? Oh come on, own up. Anyway be that as it may – CORRESPONDENCE COARSE, is a serious readers' service aimed at serious discussion of serious adult problems. (hem hem). All letters must be sincere and genuine (though not necessarily true). Please address them to: "Old Maid Only", c/o The Goodies, No Fixed Abode, Cricklewood. It is important that you include your full name and address so we know where to send the blackmail notes and so we can blame you if we get done for obscenity. However, at your request, your names will not be published unless they are particularly funny.

Unusual

Madam, Further to your correspondent F.U. who writes of erotic experiences in unusual places – I recently had a funny feeling in my big toe.
P. Brain (Notts)

Big ones

Madam, On the subject of size, Lady Grippam-Titely writes to say that she one knew a colonel in Ram Japur who had one measuring 2 feet long with a maximum circumference of 16 inches. I can well believe it – such statistics are almost commonplace amongst military men. I myself was once intimately acquainted with a lieutenant in the United States army who boasted outstanding dimensions of 3ft by 22 inches. So proud was he of his prodigious appendage, that, at the slightest encouragement he would play baseball with it. He often sported a big tin boot

on the end – which made a fearful row whenever he was roused to agitated movement; and, indeed, the noise more than once seriously threatened to divulge the rather clandestine nature of our encounters.

To be honest, impressive though it was, the beastly thing was more trouble then it was worth, It was extremely heavy. And although he would sling it over his shoulder, he, never the less, fatigued rapidly if he had to lug it for any distance. He consequently fell over a lot. Also whenever he wasn't using it, he was in the habit of leaving it dangling over the bed post – something I never really got used to.

Maybe I'm getting a bit past it, but nowadays I'm not much impressed by them – big or small. And frankly I prefer men who haven't got one at all.
Mrs. De Point (Beds)
(We are now closing this correspondence on wooden legs. No more letters on this subject please Ed).

And More on Husband Swapping

Madam, I wonder if any of your swinging readers would be interested in a little exchange deal? My husband is 5 feet 4, 12 stone and 75 years old – and I would like to swap him – for a set of airtex blankets, a portable telly and a 1873 Penny Red. Failing this, perhaps somebody would just come and take him away.

E. Bahgum (Middlesex)

A Strapping Fellow

Madam, Although I am no longer young I have by no means lost my enthusiasm for a bit of you know what.. in fact, not to mince words, I reckon I'm jolly saucy! As a matter of fact, to be honest, I can't get enough of it. What is more, I am always on the look out for "new experiences" – if you know what I mean? *(not sure yet – Ed)*

Anyway, last week I paid my usual visit to Hyde Park to feed the ducks and, dare I admit it, check out any new talent. You see, I was well aware that being a nice spring morning, the handsome inmates of the nearby Hall of Residence of the Chelsea Pensioners would be out for their constitutionals, and how right I was! You see – I have this thing about uniforms – policemen, traffic wardens, zoo keepers, lifeboatmen, Canadian mounted police – none of these are safe with me. Actually it doesn't really matter about their uniforms. Anyway that particular morning, I soon picked out a gorgeous "Old C" and in an uncontrollable surge of passion I leapt up to him and planted a big wet kiss right on his mutton chop whiskers.

Imagine my surprise when he let out a roar like a wild thing and hurled me into the long grass. But was I protesting? – not at all. I was delighted when he then leapt into the grass after me and unbuckled his belt. Imagine my surprise when he then tied my ankles securely together. Well, what a to do, I thought, but he was not finished yet – imagine my surprise when he then tore a length of braid from his uniform and securely bound my hands behind my back.

What was he going to do next? Not that I cared – I was ready for anything! But imagine my surprise when he then stuffed a roll in my mouth, then bundled me into a cardboard box and threw me in the Serpentine. Well I thought, this is a "new experience". I was scared and yet strangely excited, flushed with the anticipation of his next action. Imagine my surprise therefore, when he then ran away. Needless to say I sank to the bottom, and drowned.

I. Lovvit (Bucks)

Madam, I am not in the habit of writing to magazines such as yours. Do you realize that Blue Tits may lay as many as 12 eggs in a single nest?

Yours sincerely *(name and address witheld by request)*.
P.S. You're not really interested are you?
(No – Ed)

Madam, I am 65 years old, reasonably ugly, considerably overweight, and frequently suffer from the wind. To be perfectly honest, I do not generally enjoy any great success with the men, until last week that is. You'll never believe what happened!

It was on the Monday – no I tell a lie, it was Tuesday; I know that, 'cos we'd just been and buried our Cissy, and she'd always said she wanted to be laid under on Pancake day – well, to tell you the truth she really wanted to be cremated, but her Sidney wouldn't hear of it – anyway, I was on my way back from Sainsburys – so come to think of it must've been Thursday actually – anyway, I'll get on to the naughty bit shall I? *(Yes please – Ed)*.

O.K. here goes –

continued on page 74

THE NUDEST VICAR

Photographs by Amnon Ben-Hur

THE NUDEST VICAR

"If the Lord hadn't meant us to show them, he wouldn't have given us kneecaps." So sayeth fuzzy chopped, 36 year old Parson Snoze.

There is a ruffle of linen as he hitches up his cassock, "Too far?" he pouts. "Do carry on", we encourage him, and he does.

"I can see nothing wrong with my body" he continues. To be quite honest there are one or two things wrong with his body, but who's complaining? If he's ever going to be defrocked, send us an invite! Is he divine? We should say so . . .

Anyway, you were saying Reverend?

"I am not sectarian: Catholicism, Protestantism, Buddhism, whatever you fancy – they always fulfill the same basic human needs. I am hoping to become a model. Gosh isn't it hot in here?" Lazily he hitches up his

continued on page 74

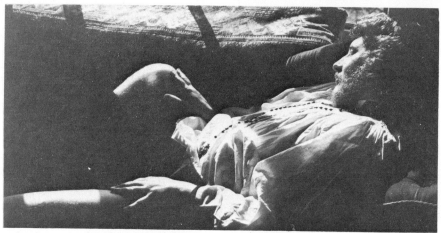

TIMONA
Our raving reporter tests the Gentry

First of all a big thank you to all of you who have come to see me at the Wind Hall Theatre, where I am currently starring in Lady Windermere's Fan (I always *knew* that title had a double meaning . . . whoops, cheeky!). My literary friends tell me that Oscar Wilde had a reputation for being a bit of a poofter; well, all I can say is he wrote some jolly saucy lines, and anyone who can create a dishy Character like Lord Darlington must have had a pretty fair idea of what a girl fancies. Does he drive *me* Wilde . . . I should say so! Anyway, don't take my word for it, ladies, you just hop along and book yourself a nice front row seat and a pair of opera glasses and have a good swoon. Oh . . . and don't bring hubby! Prices are £3, £3 and £3 . . . and there are two shows on Tuesday and Saturday. Let me know when you're coming and I'll give you a wave.

As a matter of fact being in this play (Lady Windermere's Fan, Windhall . . . remember? Tickets on sale now) gave me the idea for my present assignment. As you know, in this job, I've got around a bit . . . in fact I've got around several bits. Heaven knows I've had hot times in Hong Kong (talk about chinese crackers) and I've flirted in France (I don't mind a nibble of garlic any day) I've rubbed shoulders (and that's not all) with all types and classes from film producers to plumbers (three plumbers, if I remember rightly), BUT would you believe it, I've never so much as taken tea with a member of the aristocracy? And now, here I was night after night, parrying witticisms over the fake Wedgwood with Lord Darlington, no less. And yet, its still not the REAL thing. I mean, don't get me wrong, I've nothing against actors . . . in fact, this particular thespian is a real bundle of charm . . but that's another story (*Next week. Ed*) But there's another thing, I mean, its all very well being titillated on the proscenium every night, but performing in front of six hundred people does sort of inhibit a gal (even yours truly – and I'm hardly the shy type, as YOU know).

Anyway, I decided for my next job, I'd angle for a tangle round the tea trolley with a real live actual living (and loving!) Lord . . . and English too, of course. The last time I was at the dentist's for a new set, I was leafing through *Country Life* . . . always a classy reader me . . . when I spotted that there was to be a Royal Garden Party at Sanders (Sandringham to you, my dear). So, how to get invited? Simple . . . I got the management to slip a couple of free tickets to the Palace . . . and last Thursday matinee I knew my little ruse had worked when I saw the braided arm of a naval uniform throwing paper darts from the Royal Box. Apparently, He (no names eh?) flipped over my performance, and sure enough next day a page boy was round knocking at my penthouse door with a purple cushion, and on it . . . an invite to the Garden Party . . . with gold letters and crinkly edges – just like we've all dreamed about . . . right ladies?

Well I can tell you, I haven't been so excited since Val Doonican sent me a splinter off his rocking chair.

Sandringham is certainly the perfect setting for Romance. It is just off the A149 between Hunstanton and Kings Lynn. Not a Curlew's call away from those eery Norfolk Salt Marshes where the bittern has boomed for centuries and where wildfowlers still carry on the ancient art of punt gunning. Only the gentle whispering of the windmills' sails disturb the misty Norfolk mornings, and on the vast mudflats of the nearby Wash, the villagers still gather at dawn to dig out cockles and lugworms. But who cares? Such thoughts were hardly in MY mind as I arrived at the Garden Party. "So," I thought, "this is where the nobs hang out." In no time at all I was surrounded by dishy men of every shape, size and colour. "Wow," I thought, "If I'd started out here, I could have avoided all that travelling." There were super male specimens from all over the world . . . and all of them classy with it! In the space of two minutes, I'd been slipped a cucumber sandwich by the Spanish Ambassador, halved a muffin with a Prince from Basutoland, and accepted a very suggestive chipolata from the King of Thailand. "But enough of these foreign *hors d'oeuvres*," I said to myself, "Timona my girl, you've got a job to do." And it was tea I was after . . .

and that means English tea, served by an Englishman, the way only Englishmen can.

Anyway, at that moment, I spotted the gent in the naval uniform striding across the lawn with his two huge sunburnt hands clasped behind his back. God, how I LOVE expressive hands! And wow! were his expressive! With just the merest gesture of two fingers he indicated that I should pursue my investigation elsewhere. A lady with my experience knows when to take a hint, and anyway, today I was only after a Lord . . . not Royalty, and in any case, that's another story (*Two weeks time. Ed*) So . . . I quickly turned away and tripped over the Foreign Secretary . . . it was as I was being helped to my feet that I spied HIM. THIS was the one . . . and I knew it! He must've been at least six foot tall; though it wasn't too easy to judge with him being all hunched up in his bathchair. But clearly he was every inch a Lord . . . from the top of his coronet to the tip of his wooden leg (And I don't care what Mrs De Point says, *I* like them, and the bigger the better!)

He was fast asleep, and so I was able to stare at him through my binoculars without unduly embarrassing him. He clearly wasn't a young man . . in fact, for a moment I wasn't sure if he was still alive. And yet, from the rakish angle at which he's draped his tartan blanket – exposing just a smidgeon of one knee (he only had one knee) I was willing to bet he was young at heart! One glance at his flies told me he was a fisherman, and instantly I knew how I was going to make him *my* catch.

I leapt into the ladies loo, pausing only to snaffle a plateful of salmon sandwiches. When I want something (or someone!) I have no shame about using all my womanly wiles to get it. Within minutes I would make myself irresistable to the noble Lothario.

With no thought for modesty, I

unbuttoned my choker collar to half an inch below the neckline; I strung up my corset a couple more notches; and I shed two of my six petticoats. Almost frantically I stuffed them into my hand bag. Lord . . . if he'd only known! . . there was nothing between him and the REAL ME . . . but one layer of harris tweed, four of imitation terylene, two of canvas and one of reinforced blue flannelette! I felt deliciously naughty! Then, for the final touch . . . I took out the filling from the salmon sandwiches and squeezed the fishy juice all over me . . . taking care not to miss those "intimate areas" . . . round my ankles and up my nose.

Then I emerged. The effect was devastating. Instantly my lovely lord leapt to his foot. His nurse was sent sprawling, and his blanket fell to the floor, revealing that tell-tale bulge in his trousers that means so much to yours truly . . . I ADORE pipe smokers! Then his fisherman's nostrils quivered as he sniffed the salmon. With a groan of passion he fell on me. As I helped him up, he ecstatically recalled how he'd landed a twelve pounder up the Wye Valley. He was hooked!

As you know, I'm not one of those ladies who beat about the bush, I knew what I wanted and I was going to get it. And how! As I tucked him back in his bathchair, I came straight to the point. "How about a cuppa tea, then?" He needed no further prompting. Instantly he'd called for a new pot.

Now I know that some women prefer to lead in these matters, but not yours truly. If the fella wants to be "mother" thats O.K. by me. Theres nothing I like better than having my cup filled by a handsome hunk of man. And could he pour? Oh boy . . . I should say SO! From fully eighteen inches above the cup, straight in, and no mistake! And no instant quick brew for him . . . he took his time! When it came to the sugar lumps, he flicked them in from his waist like Tony Jacklin sinking a putt. And when he stirred. Oh I thought I'd pass out. Not the quick flick most men give it . . . but long slow sweeping circles that spoke of years of breeding! I was lapping it up. I make a lot of noise when I drink tea. Heaven knows I enjoy it . . . and I'm not ashamed to let it show. Some men might be put off . . . but not HIM. Every slurp seem to spur him on. As fast as I drank . . . he poured . . . And I'll tell you, each cup was more satisfying than the last.

It wasn't until we'd drunk, oh, maybe four or five pots full – and big English pots too . . . that we were both satiated. Talk about My Sweet Lord . . . I should say so!

What a pity he had to go and spoil it all by suggesting we follow it up by nipping off to the bushes for a quick . . .

continued on page 74

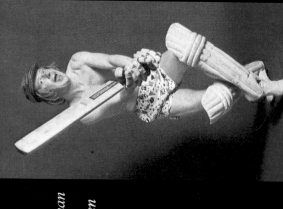

Mr March

*Mr. March is
willing to show
Exactly where the
March winds
blow!*

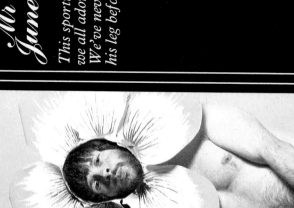

Mr June

*This sporting man
we all adore,
We've never seen
his leg before!*

Mr February

*Mr. Feb. is quite
divine,
He is your special
valentine!*

Mr May

*This is the time for
flowers gay,
And here's a pansy
– Mr. May!*

Mr January

*The snow may
snow, the storm
may storm,
But Mr. Jan. is
always warm!*

Mr April

*The April showers
came your way,
And who's this
drip? – it's Mr. A!*

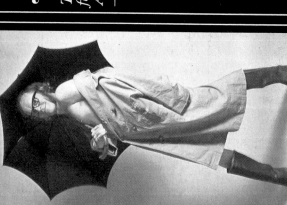

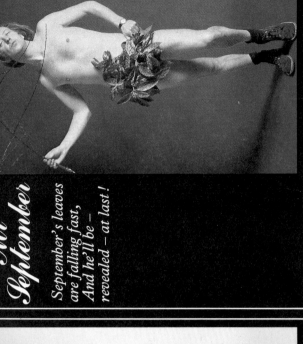

Mr September

September's leaves
are falling fast,
And he'll be –
revealed – at last !

Mr December

Mr D. is always
Jolly,
But careful where
you put the holly !

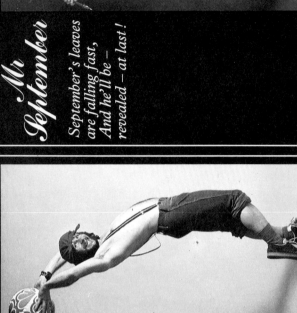

Mr August

Holiday time for
one and all,
And Mr. August
has a ball !

Mr November

This Guy is full of
fire,
When he's alight
you'd best retire !

Mr July

The 4th, it is
Thanksgiving
Day,
And we give
thanks for Mr. J !

Mr October

A hunting man is
Mr. O,
Just crack the
whip and watch
him go !

P.S. Hope you last the year!

Continued from page 1
...rubbish

YOUR EDITOR.

Continued from page 2
...no, I tell a lie, it was Friday. Anyway I must fly I've got a shank in the oven.

MISS T. F. (OXON).

Continued from page 56
...game of polo.

TIMONA.

Continued from page 42
...come to think of it, I wasn't surprised at all.

(Name address withheld).

Continued from page 14
...half a dozen eggs and a pound of Phillipino lard. Amazing what some people get up to, isn't it?

MISS FITT (Lancs).

Continued from page 38
...THE END.

SAUCI-AID. LTD,
Give Nature a Leg Up!

There comes a time in everyone's life when we have to admit that we are "not quite what we were." BUT this is absolutely no reason why this should spell the end of sauciness in YOUR life (or ours, for that matter). Each of our products is scientifically designed (by master carpenters, Ford-car workers, & Clydeside ship builders), to give YOU the extra support that nature, perhaps, is failing to provide these days.

SCAFFOLDING

PROPS

Make your SAUCINESS MORE ENJOYABLE MORE SATISFYING

SPLINTS

Medically Approved

BLINDFOLDS

"When Faculties fade Use a SAUCI—AID"

Write to Sauci-Aid Ltd, Cricklewood, for full Catalogue.

NEW also from SAUCI–AID

FOR HIM *Gigolo* **FALSE MOUSTACHES.**

A NEW MAN in your life every day!

A Gigolo moustaches Tickles – YOUR fancy!

"Spanking Colonel"   "Young Raver"   "Fuzzy Chops"

PLUS
"Suggestive" – false eyebrows.

"Valentino" Teeth
"Wicked Grin Mk II"

For a smile YOU cannot resist . . .

PERSONALIZED STONE HOT WATER BOTTLE

How would you like YOUR favourite man curled up on your knee? He can be, whenever you use a "PERSONALITY" Stone Hotty.

Who do YOU fancy?
Nicholas Parsons?   Hughie Green?
Max Bygraves?   Des O' Connor? –
have you NO taste!??

OPENING SHORTLY
THE NEW – OLD MAID CLUB

Old maid is proud to announce that we have managed to combine funds with the Cricklewood Womens Institute to secure the premises of the 14th N. London Boy's Brigade Hall, on Tuesdays and Thursdays (after Kung Fu Classes) for our new.EXCLUSIVE – OLD MAID CLUB

TIMONA says GOSH – this too, is a bit cheeky

IT'S SAUCY

And
Old Maid Only goes INTER-NATIONAL. Opening shortly Old Maid Clubs in

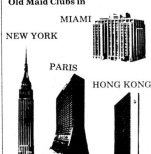

MIAMI

NEW YORK

PARIS

HONG KONG

1. *Hilton Hotel Florida*
2. *Empire state Building*
3. *The Louvres*
4. *Hong Kong Playboy club.*

3 BARS!
Get a bit tiddly at any one of three bars (they are situated next to one another due to pressure of space) . . .

GAMES ROOM
. . . or relax in the exclusive games room (same place as the 3 bars) – Bingo – Gin Rummy – Whist & Bridge – or for the more energetic – Lewdo . . .

DISCO
or Dance under the flashing lights (optical treatment available at nearby clinic) in the Dance Hall (situated in the Games Room).

And every month – A LIVE GROUP! (well, they were alive last time we saw them). The saucy rhythms of the Henry Hall orchestra.*

This is not THE HENRY HALL orchestra.

Wild Nights At The Club!

We have managed to secure a special license extension, which allows us to stay open till 7.30 p.m. (Last drinks 7.00)

ALL NIGHT (till 7.30 anyway) you will be pampered by our outrageous saucy "OLD MAID ONLY" WOLVES.

See them do the delicate and ever so slightly wicked – "WOLF DIP" – as they serve YOUR table.

GRRR!! I'M A WOLF.

Plus SWIMMING POOL
(only 5 mins down the road, No 65 bus direct to Municipal Baths, Cricklewood Broadway).

DARE YOU WEAR THESE!?

MAKE BED-TIME, BAD-TIME – with SAUCI-TOGS LTD.

"Shorty Nightie" 7 inches from the ground!

"Who's a big boy then," LONG JOHNS with see through knee panels

"Scamp" string vest with extra big holes reveals almost everything!

"Knaughty-Knicks"

"Scanti-Briefs!" He'll feel like a tiger!

'Saucebox' Surgical Bedsox

THEY'RE TOO MUCH OR TOO LITTLE

'Rip Van Twinkle' Nightcap

"Caution"

"Peepitoes" open toed slippers – give just a tantalising glimpse

Write for catalogue to The House of Sauci-Togs, Cricklewood.

Daily ~ Mail
WEDNESDAY, APRIL 30, 1975   6p (CHANNEL ISLANDS 7p)

1g

JUDGE RAPS GOODIES

By our rather special correspondent

THE GOODIES LIBEL TRIAL, as it is being called, moved into a new phase today as the plaintiffs, the Goodies themselves, brought their own case to a close.

Now it is up to Weidenfeld and Nicolson the defendants to disprove the allegations of libel brought against them by the Goodies.

And frankly, who cares? I know you don't, and neither would I if I wasn't getting paid for writing about it. Actually, I'm getting paid a fair bit, and I *still* don't care. By the way, the headline isn't my idea – just one of our sub-editors out for an easy-to-read attention-getting phrase that has nothing to do with anything in the article. Still, what the hell, nobody reads this muck anyway, and even if they do they don't take it in

love is...

review
view bo...   now   ids,
warmly,
tension lu...   esh   a
the shades...   was
flick and tu...   dn't
the edge to...   ould
"I'm ve...   ould   ause
with a n...   hese
people say...   heir
that book...
further fro...   left
written for...   ish
body."   it
He's eve...   ry
himself so...   ul.
what the   ere
want to kn...
"I mean...
to people
once ever.
particular
do it again
have give
it's very d...
days. Peo...
own arses
"I figur...
was esse...
everybody

The Harlesden Advertiser and Courier

Personality Page

ONE TIME VISITOR to Harlesden, Rick Bronson, has a friend known as Big Syd who met an acquaintance who actually was present at the controversial Goodies libel trial today. According to Rick's chum's pal, things began to look better when exhibit K was produced by Mr Brooke-Taylor (no Harlesden connections!) during cross examination to prove that the Goodies were capable of providing literary work of a competent and educational standard.

Another personality in the news who has not yet visited Harlesden is Leonid Brezhnev, the Russian politician, who only recently announced

after his im-
life, has him
live luxuri-
I'm on tour
necessitates
-five gigs in
gotta live
utta that in
ey you can
Concorde
ou'll be able
alf hours of
iving well is
ng to do. My
, I wanna
, I wanna
na car. I
ared to say.
gs."
discovered
ere are few
th.
different
I move in.
er."
superstar
e it. Fancy
clique – it

w. I can go
thousand
problems
th a guy –
ow than I
especiall
e same,
I liste
r p...

The Crystal Ball
Official Publication of the Clairvoyant Association
(Founded 1957 – Disbanded 1994)

SENSATION IN COURT

TODAY THE GOODIES appear to have succeeded in disproving the accusations made against them of being loonies, thick as three short planks, behind the times, disreputable etc etc.

Tomorrow, the publishers Weidenfeld and Nicolson will attempt to discredit the Goodies, but without success. The day after, their counsel, a tall dark stranger named Eamonn dePinn QC, will cut himself shaving, than take a journey across tarmac to the courtroom. There he will make an utter fool of himself and be shouted at by the judge. He will produce a surprise

cause half the western

witness (Mr Point-Compleatly) but will fail to impress the jury. The following afternoon, the judge will decide against buying the pink wallpaper for the upstairs dining room, and go for the imitation Yak-skin wall covering instead. He will then go home and mow the dog. Several years later, he will emigrate to South Africa, and live to a ripe old age – more ripe than old. Also on the horizon I see

...era of organised
...he reigned; not
...ine, but the perfect ambas-
...ador of a life-style as distinct
from the masses as ours is now' –
so might his biography read in
the library of some futuristic
cosmos.

RACING NEWS

Tomorrow's results
at Kempton Park

3.30

1 ... Wounded Nun – 11-1
2 ... Salty Wombat – 13-8
3 ... Funky Gibbon – 17 - 5¾
                20 - 1 Bar

or
be
pe...
is
dai
gen
side
Le
Ever
for th...
that e...
extra f...
that is
all about.

Please send fre...

Name ....

Address ....

under the ag...
apart f...

GOODY GOODY !!

JULY 21ST — EVERY SATURDAY — 3½p

THE COMIT FOR **NICE CLEAN WELL-BEHAVED** CHILDREN!

BOFFO THE BORE

'ELLO PALS!

WOW! LOOK AT THIS—A BANANA SKIN LEFT CARELESSLY LYING ON THE GROUND!

AND HERE COMES FARMER GILES WITH **TEN** DOZEN EGGS! GUESS WHAT'S GOING TO HAPPEN NEXT!

THAT'S RIGHT—I'M GOING TO PREVENT A NASTY SLIP-UP!

THINKS: THAT WAS FUN!

NOT WHISTLING

NOT IN POCKETS

NICE AND SHINY

TO CHURCH

WOULD YOU BELIEVE IT!. TSK TSK! SOME STUPID PERSON HAS UNTIDILY LEFT A **SWEETIE** ON THE PATH!

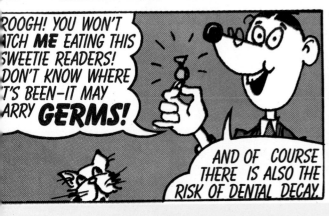

ROOGH! YOU WON'T CATCH **ME** EATING THIS SWEETIE READERS! I DON'T KNOW WHERE IT'S BEEN—IT MAY CARRY **GERMS!**

AND OF COURSE THERE IS ALSO THE RISK OF DENTAL DECAY.

I'M TAKING IT TO THE POLICE-STATION

LATER

WELL, I CERTAINLY PICKED UP A THING OR TWO TODAY! NOW I'D BETTER HURRY OFF HOME— IT'S TIME FOR A LOVELY WASH!   GOODBYE ALL!

LOTS MORE FUN INSIDE WITH *Dennis the Vicar!*

MERRY GRAEME'S PAGE OF PHACTS 'N' PHUN!

Hi folks!

GOODIES SECRET CODE

AN OPTICAL ILLUSION!

WHICH LINE IS THE LONGER?

THEY MAY LOOK THE SAME — BUT IN FACT THEY ARE DIFFERENT LENGTHS.

HERE IS A MESSAGE IN GOODIES SECRET CODE:

"BOTXFS PO QBHF OJOFUZ-FJHIU"

(ANSWER ON PAGE NINETY-EIGHT)

AMAZE YOUR DAD AND MUM!

COME DOWN TO BREAKFAST DRUNK

let's talk **COCKNEY RHYMING SLANG!**

says **COCKNEY SID** A WORKING-CLASS PERSON.

HELP LITTLE BONGO THE ELF GET TO THE LAVATORY.

WOTCHER MATES! US COCKNEY SPARRERS IS ALLUS USING THIS 'ERE RHYMING SLANG — AND YOU CAN DO IT AN' ALL! "APPLES AND PEARS" MEANS STAIRS! SEE? EASY INNIT? WELL, HERE'S SOME MORE ~

APPLES AND STRIFE — WIFE
APPLES AND FLUTE — SUIT
APPLES AND PINNER — DINNER
APPLES AND COMBAT — WOMBAT
APPLES AND CURLY THING — PEARLY KING.

CHEERIO CHUMS!

BEST SELLERS

English.

1 "Was God an English Astronaut?" Tim Brooke-Taylor.

2 "Noddy goes to the lavatory."
Enid Blightown.

3 "Jewish Trees".   Weidenfelds.

4 "My Favourite Herbs."
Fanny Cradock.
(Sequel to 'Freds I have loved')

Scottish.

1 "Was God a Scottish Astronaut?"
Tim McBrooke-Taylor.

2 "Up the Rangers."
a history of Rangers Football Club.

3 "Right Up the Rangers."
a history of Celtic Football Club.

In UK only
£4.50

JACKET DESIGN BY
HARDY AMIES.

"Was God an English Astronaut? Don't make me laugh."
THE OBSERVER

"It don't make me laugh either."
A. J. P. TAYLOR, SUNDAY EXPRESS

"The biggest load of . . . . incredible . . . . facts . . . . ever published."
NEW STATESMAN

"I can . . . . possibly recommend it to anyone."
GRAEME GREENE. (Postman)

"Well . . . . me!"
BILL ODDIE

"Stranger things have happened."
JIMMY SAVILE O.B.E.

"The public must be very gullible. Thank goodness."
ERIC VON DANIKEN.

Weidenfeld & Nicolson

WAS GOD AN ENGLISH ASTRONAUT

Unsolved mysteries of the past

Tim Brooke-Taylor

They laughed at Galileo, they laughed at Newton, they even laughed at Jimmy Tarbuck – but will they laugh at Tim Brooke-Taylor?

Mr Brooke-Taylor has written a short, easy to read and controversial book. (Ideal for exclusive extracts in the Sunday Papers. For easy terms contact Weidenfeld or Nicolson).

It will shock, it will astound, but above all it will sell *your* newspaper.

This major work is humbly dedicated to Her Majesty, The Queen

PREFACE

It took courage to write this book, and it will take courage to read it. Some people won't like it, but they'll probably be Wops, Frogs, Krauts or Welshmen.

This book could hurt some people, but not much as it's quite short and light.

Lack of space stops me from mentioning everyone who has helped, but I would just like to thank Dr Garden for his Foreward, and Christine who toped the manuscript.

Tim Brooke-Taylor, Cricklewood 1975.

FOREWARD

When I first read the manuscript I thought it was a load of old drivel. But then something that Tim said made me change my mind. I now think that this is probably the most important piece of writing to have emerged in the last million years, and is undoubtedly the work of a genius.

May Hippocrates forgive me.

Dr Graeme Garden, Cricklewood 1975.

First Published . . . . June 1975
Roprunted . . . . . June 1975
Raprented . . . . . June 1975
Reprintud . . . . . June 1975
xjpRiqltd . . . . . June 1975
Reprinted . . . . . June 1974

Damn!
That'll do Ed.

CHAPTER 1

ENGLAND'S GREEN AND PLEASANT LANDING FIELD.

England has been the focus of Alien landings for hundreds, if not thousands of years. This is the inescapable fact that has emerged after painstaking research spread over several days.

I shall produce photographs and reports of many different sightings of Alien space-ships that have taken place within the last few years – all of them in North London (Cricklewood actually). If we take this small area as a typical cross section, then space-ship arrivals have taken on the proportion of an inter-planetary rush hour. I contend that England is the King's Cross of the Universe.

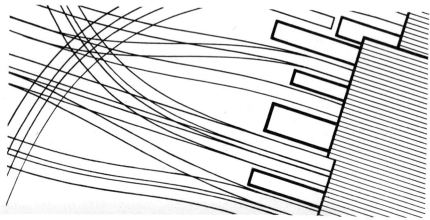

CHAPTER 2

SING A SONG OF SPACE CRAFT.

Ancient man through buildings, legends and nursery rhymes has handed down his experience of 'landings' that have taken place over the millenia.

Little Miss Muffet sat on a tuffet,
Eating her curds and wey.
Down came a spider
Who sat down beside her,
And frightened Miss Muffet away.

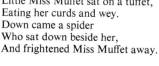

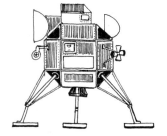

A spider   **Moon landing vehicle**

Not to mention 'four and twenty blackbirds'.

A blackbird

CHAPTER 3

THE FLAMING PUDDING.

The early Christian missionaries to England, as we know, adapted an ancient feastival and made it Christmas. The ancient feastival itself must surely have been the celebration of a 'god' and his 'landing'.

A tree   or   A rocket?

The coincidence is too much to accept. The star we have always assumed was the Star of Bethlehem. Could it not symbolise the destination of the rocket/tree?

A plum pudding   A flying saucer

We pour brandy on the plum pudding and light it. Why? I suggest that this represents the heat haze that must have accompanied the flight of such a space vehicle.

A Christmas snowman usually thought of as just a childish recreation. I'm not so sure.

A snowman
or
a . . .

CHAPTER 4

THE CHURCH: A SPACE MUSEUM?

Many of our cathedrals are a beauty in their own right. A tribute to God. But are they something more?

A cathedral

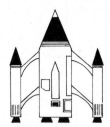

Space vehicle

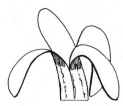

A peeled banana

A gargoyle on Winchester Cathedral

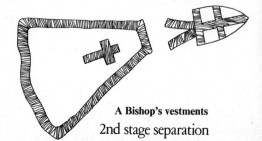

A Bishop's vestments

2nd stage separation

CHAPTER 5

WAS GOD AN ENGLISH RUGGER INTERNATIONAL?

In many instances of sightings U.F.O.'s have been described as cigar shaped, or as I would have it, 'Rugby football shaped!'

England h
thousands of y
painstaking rese
I shall prod
Alien space-ship
in North Lond
typical cross sect
an inter-planeta
the Universe.

The goals

Reminiscent of something? Of course: a television aerial. An obvious sign of an advanced civilization.

The scrum

The spider

A moon landing vehicle

CHAPTER 6

OR WAS HE A CRICKETER?

Is it a coincidence that the early cricketers played with a wicket that had two stumps and one bail?

Not a far cry from the mysterious stones of Stonehenge, or indeed the mathematical mystery to end all mysteries $\pi(r^2)$ Not to mention a letter box Coincidence? I rather think not.

CHAPTER 7

THE BOWLER HAT CONTROVERSY

For years sociologists have argued over the Englishman's use of the bowler hat. Why wear something so impractical? The answer is perhaps deeper even than they imagined:

Bowler hat

Spaceship

The Priest's Hat from Italy

and the Mexican Sombrero

The last two provide a confusion. But perhaps this can be explained by space-ships that mistook Italy and Mexico for England. A mistake that can be forgiven in a vessel that has travelled billions of light years. (The Mexican Hat Dance would provide an interesting study. For surely there is more to life than jumping on hats – even for Mexicans).
None of this, of course, explains the orange squeezer:

CHAPTER 8

THE LOCH NESS MONSTER FROM OUTER SPACE.

All of us, I am sure, have climbed out of our baths causing water to fly from our bodies and form pools on the bathroom floor. If we are to suppose that a rocket rises from the ocean bed, just off the coast of Scotland, then water would be splashed on to the land causing "bathroom pools". One such pool, I contend, is Loch Ness. Contained within this water would undoubtedly be some living organism which has been washed off the space-ship's shell. An organism that has survived the journey through space from some distant planet. Over thousands of years this organism will have evolved into the creature we know as the Loch Ness Monster.

The Loch Ness Monster

Railway bridge

Three elephants at a water hole

CHAPTER 11

For ye
bowler hat.
deeper even

Bowler hat

The Priest's H

and the Mexic

The las
space-ships
be forgiven
Hat Dance
life than jun
None of thi:
explains the

TH

All of ι
from our bc
that a rock
water woul
such pool,
undoubtedl;
ship's shell.
some distan
into the crea

The ea
ancient fea:
surely have

A tree or A

The co
was the Sta
rocket/tree?

We po
this represe
space vehic

**John Cowan, Surplus Cadaver Operative.
(Undertaker)**

'It was a Thursday, I know because Mrs Polegrease had just passed away. I was preparing her casket when I saw this incredible sight. "Good Grief" I thought, that being the motto of our firm, "This must be the end, I'm beginning to see things" and started at once to prepare a casket for myself. I took a photo, but never expected it to come out.'

**Nathaniel Smalls, Rodent Operative.
(Rat Catcher)**

'On the ground was an object like a cigar tube, and around it was scorched earth. A small creature was emerging. I'd never seen anything like it before. I smelt a rat, but then that's my job. I let it go as it was my day off. 'It' let out a strange high-pitched squeak which sounded like: "That's one small step for a Martian. A giant leap for Martiankind". Unfortunately, at that moment, I accidentally squashed it with my foot.'

**Brian Carter, God Operative.
(Vicar)**

I was looking up at the church steeple wondering how much longer it would stay up, when I saw something most strange – something that could only be described as a flying tea-cup. "Good Lord" I thought, but then that's my job. Fortunately I had my Instamatic with me, so I took a quick snap. Thank goodness I did, for at that moment the steeple collapsed. Contributions please to: Church Restoration Fund, St Edna's, Cricklewood.

Before

After

George Weidenfeld and Nicolson Limited

Weiden, Feld or Nicolson

now at: "Dunpublishing" The Back of Boots Ruislip Somerset *Telephone* 01-228 8888

Registered number 395166 England *Telegrams and cables* Nicobar London SW11 1XA *Telex* 918066

Tim Brooke-Taylor Esq.,

No Fixed Abode

Nr. Cricklewood

London

PR1 DE   12th inst.

Dear Mr. Brooke-Taylor,

      Due to a lack of interest in your book, "The Chariot
of the Dogs", we have decided not to publish.

      Instead we are going to use the paper for a new manuscript
we have received from a Mrs. E. Tole., entitled The Goodies File.

                 Yours sincerely

Ethel Weidenfeld

             Ethel Weidenfeld

Was God a ssian Spy sing as an nglish stronaut?"

Tim Brooke-Taylor's
amazing discovery

:he ground was an object like a

colc
an
cor
Op
acr
cor
sen
arn
mu
the
sayin
Apple
"It's a
you c
reaso
gives
occasi

inclusive arrangements offering
two nights in a room with a
bathroom at the famous Dicken-

regretted the fu
fast I had wol

Coming Soon
"Charriots of the Dogs"
by
Tim Brooke-Taylor

The first space
travellers were
dogs – amazing new
theories by the author of:
"was God an English Astronaut"

rprisingly, the ultra-earthy Lexy believes that you can c

Chairman and Joint Managing Director Sir George Weiden
Deputy Chairman John Weidenfeld *Joint Managing Director* Steven Weidenfeld *Assistant Managing Director and Comp* villag
Directors Stewart Weidenfeld Mavis Weidenfeld Jim Weidenfeld Jeremy Weidenfeld (deceased)
Michael Weidenfeld Bill Weidenfeld Fingers Weidenfeld Doreen Weidenfeld Nigel Weidenfeld Ethel Weidenfeld

VOGUE

Law Report

THE GOODIES vs WEIDENFELD PUBS.

FAR-FETCHED

Descriptions of the Goodies' publication "Was God an English Astronaut?" as being "utterly unbelievable" dismissed as "Far-Fetched" by Mr Justice I. Thort in today's instalment of this sensational trial – sensational partly due to the *exceptional* dress sense of the leading legal lights. The judge himself was devastating in carefully chosen co-ordinates, boldly mixing scarlet and black to offset a bold grey rinse which somehow *made sense* of otherwise eccentric styling of his shoulder length hair – (a wig perhaps?) – though let it be said that it was somehow necessary for such a statement of *chic* to excuse his choice of a full-length gown for so businesslike an occasion.

LOAD OF OLD RUBBISH

Speaking on behalf of the defendants, however, Mr Lars Buster-Peckham, QC, insisted that the Judge's suggestion that descriptions

of the Goodies' book as being "utterly unbelievable" were "[far] fetched" was "a load of old rubbish." The short grey pigtails wh[ich] served to offset his sober black gown were echoed jauntily in t[he] perky little white cravat sprouting so cheekily from beneath [his] dimpled chin. Nice. (His briefs, pale beige of course, were secur[ed] by a pink ribbon.) So satisfactory, one thought, to see a member [of] the legal profession not only so aware of the importance of on[e's] choice of clothes, but also as camp as old boots.

POSING

Here I was jerked back to reality by Mr Oddie who leapt to his f[eet] announcing that if the Goodies were so disreputable, then why wa[s it] that when the Government were in a spot of bother, "they alwa[ys] called on us, the Goodies? Eh? Eh? Answer me that mate! Y[es] Abababa – *you* listen mate! Eh? Yes! Oh yes etc etc." (Mr Od[die] was wearing a mauve posing vest with matching *continued page 2[0]*

EXHIBIT L

TOP SECRET FILE

Title. *The Crisis File*

PRAVDA

Britain харьковских партийных, советских и про-
фессиональных crisis построить в Харькове,
столице Советской Украины, здание для государ-
ственного Chancellor of The Exchequor театра масс
неразрывно связано с ростом украинской пролетарской государственности и Funny Farm культур-
грандиозного подъема социалистической индустр
укрепления пролетарской диктатуры, социалист-
ского преобразования сельского хозяйства. ● Ре-
структивный desperate народного хозяйства
есть в то же время период бурного развёрты
культурной революции. Tee! Hee!
тельства культурных. Tee! Hee!
альной основы для дальнейшего роста
по форме и пролетарской
ской культуры является
ших задач реконструк-
революция и социа-
вая широчайшие
областях

TIMES

Daily Mirror
EUROPE'S BIGGEST DAILY SALE
5p Thursday, January 16, 1975

CRISIS

£5 £10 £14 £24 £54 £3000?
JAN FEB MARCH APRIL MAY JUNE
YOUR MONTHLY FOOD BILL

MONTHLY FOOD BILL £5 TO £24!

FINANCIAL

Pound Collaps

THE Sun
FORWARD WITH THE PEOPLE
Thursday, January 30, 1975

FUEL CUTS TO COME

Daily Telegraph

PRICES UP UP UP

EXPRESS
Weather: Cloudy, some rain
WHAT NOW P.M

THE GOODIES

No Fixed Abode, Nr. Cricklewood, London

April, 12th inst.

Dear Prime Minister,

We wondered if the enclosed clippings might be of some interest to you. We realize that you are jolly busy, and might not always have time to read the papers, so we are sending you these in case you missed them. We think you must've missed them, otherwise you would have done something about them by now. Anyway, we feel that we should point out, if you don't mind, that headlines like these do not do your reputation any good. Heaven knows we realize you can't work miracles - but you can't expect ordinary people to understand that - especially when you say to them that you can.

Anyway, if you don't mind us giving you a bit of friendly advice - strictly off the record, and no price to pay, of course - we reckon that you ought to solve Britain's Economic Crisis as soon as possible; otherwise people are bound to go off you a bit (no offence meant, Sir). We apologise if you have already thought of this. Looking forward to an early reply.

Love,

The Goodies

THE GOODIES
p.s. We think you're clever
p.p.s. No taxes on three-seater bikes eh eh?..

HOUSE OF COMMONS
LONDON SWIA OAA

Number 10

Mon. 16th Inst.

Dear Goodies,

            Thanks for the cuttings. Gosh, I hadn't realized! I mean,
what with falling out of boats, writing memoirs and lighting my pipe,
things can slip your mind. Well, they certainly slipped mine! Anyway,
I've been doing a spot of checking up - the country is in a bit of a
pickle isn't it? I've got to admit, we don't seem to have an awful lot
in the old coffers...in fact we're flipping skint. Thank heavens you
pointed it out...perhaps it's not too late. Well my Government and I have
been having a fair old rabbit about it, and this morning we came to the
reluctant decision that we have no option but to sell the Queen. You may
wonder how Her Majesty's Government can sell Her Majesty...well, I think
I already have done! You'll be pleased to hear I've had a very reasonable
offer from Walt Disney Productions, who want to dismantle Her, and the
Palace, and reconstruct them in California. She rather fancies the idea!
Unfortunately, the price is nowhere near good enough to clear our debts -
and well, a Royal Family is not much cop without its titular head is it?-
so I've come to the conclusion that I may as well sell the rest of them
as well. To be honest, I've had this one in mind for a while, and I've
been dropping the odd word round the International Conferences and Clubs
etc., but I'm afraid there's not been a lot of interest; except of course,
from General Amin, who's willing to buy the kids. I've told him there's no
meat on them, but he never listens to anyone. But as for the rest...not a
nibble! Anyway, I've decided to put them up for auction, but I can't
really bank on getting a decent price - so...I'm going to sell the Cabinet
as well, and the Junior Ministers, and well..in short..the whole flippin'
Government! I only hope the Opposition will be sporting enough to put
themselves on offer too, otherwise I'm going to look a right chump! Oh, and
I'm also flogging off a few Counties, Towns etc. etc. - Won't bore you
with the details: The whole shabang goes under the hammer at Sotheby's
next Thursday. I enclose a catalogue. Don't let anyone else see it, or it
might cause a bit of a stink, and I can't stand another fuss. Good God!
I'm just about to be sold - I hope - so I think I deserve a lay-off from
aggro for a few days.

                    Thanks again, and I hope you approve.

                    Yours

                    Harold

        Prime Minister

P.S. If you fancy anything - or anyone - on sale, I'm sure we can 'come to
an arrangement' if you give me a call.

SOTHEBY'S
GRAND SALE

Official Catalogue

Thursday 26th Inst. 1975

LOTS 1, 2, 3, 4, 5, 6, 7, 8, and 9

This lot may be purchased as a set, or individually. Sheer unabashed luxury. Beautifully finished – in ermine, gold etc. Of no great practical value, but immensely endearing and certainly impressive to emergent nations, Australians, grannies etc. etc.

LOT 10

This highly desirable family residence – at present the occasional town house of LOTS 1, 2, 3, 4, 5, 6, 7, 8, and 9 – will in fact, comfortably accomodate about 500 people. Full C.H complete with fixtures and fittings and 59 Horse guards. Inside lavatory. Own large garden. Very convenient for West End, theatres, shops etc.

NB
* Procedure for bidding :-
* Bidders are requested to raise one hand or one left leg behind your midd N-- ticks are advised Anyone w--- Management is no---
No cheque---

LOT 11

'The Cabinet'
Purchaseable only as a set. A good buy' for any country fancying a crac-- 'independence'?

LOT 12

A genuine 'primitive' with a rough ch-- all of its own. Several previous own-- Probably could do with a 'de-coke'; reasonable offer refused.

LOT 13

'The Lords'
Priceless antiques.
They simply so not make them like t-- anymore.

LOT 14

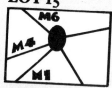

Lancashire
Conveniently situated on fly-lines fro-- America. Black pudding, trips, comedia-- and Coronation Street etc. endless amuse-- ment to transatlantic visitors. Could mak-- ideal 51st state.

LOT 15

Birmingham
Birmingham may not be much to look at-- but its happy dark-skinned inhabitant-- make it potentially Europe's answer t-- Barbados.

LOT 16

The North Sea
An aqua-paradise! Excellent swimming, boating, fishing, oil, gas and private radio-- stations.

THE GOODIES
No Fixed Abode, Nr. Cricklewood, London

Dear P.M.,

                                                17th inst.
Always knew you were a flipping loony! Thank you for your letter - we don't think. Tim hasn't stopped crying since it arrived. What are you? Man or monster? Honestly! We're beginning to wonder if it's only St Bruno you smoke in that silly pipe! Anyway you must not, repeat not, sell England, or any part of it. You just tell Sotheby's it's all off.
We can only assume that you were trying to annoy us so that we'd come up with a better idea.
Dear, dear.....why can't you just ask? Too pig-headed-North-Country-proud,we suppose.
Alright.....just give us a couple of days and we'll sort it all out for you.
God Save the Queen, Rule Britannia etc.

Yours,

The Goodies

The Goodies
p.s. How much do you want for Westminster Abbey?

SHORTAGES ETC

Food Supply: Hungry mouths to feed...

There simply is not enough food to go round. This is because everyone eats too much. We therefore suggest the introduction of a Fat Tax. Everyone will be allowed twenty pounds of weight for every inch of height: anything over that, and you'll be liable to be taxed at 10p in the pound (weight). So it will pay you all to remain small and thin, which, in turn, will help our transport problem insofar as more people will be able to cram into a bus, meaning we'll need less buses.

Even so, you will all have to tighten your belts – otherwise your trousers will fall down – 'cos you've got so thin. The minute your trousers do fall down, you will become liable to an Indecent Exposure Tax. We are not against indecent exposure – in fact, we rather enjoy it – but, in future, you will have to pay for our pleasures.

We are also very concerned to stop the population explosion, people found exploding will be stopped.

At present the average family contains two children.

We want to cut this average down by just over a half. In future it will be illegal to have more than seven-eighths of a child. Parents will, of course, be allowed to decide which bit is missing. Here are some suggestions:

Housing and Transport

There is at present a serious lack of housing. Cities such as Birmingham, Manchester and Glasgow are very overcrowded.

Meanwhile, we are spending millions of pounds on motorways, most of which lead to London. We propose to move the entire populations of Birmingham, Manchester and Glasgow to London. Once we've done that, we can scrap the motorways. And what's more, Birmingham, Manchester and Glasgow will have lots of empty houses for people to move into.

Defence

In one fell swoop we intend to cut back all our defence expenses by abolishing the entire military force and all its equipment and replacing them with a white flag.

BROADCASTING

Reorganization of the BBC

First some good news: the price of a TV set will be reduced to £10. Licences, however, will have to be increased to £350. This is not as bad as it seems since, owing to economy measures, there's not likely to be anything on worth watching.

We have already received the following statement from the BBC's Controller of Programs:

BBC TELEVISION CENTRE

Dear Goodies,

The BBC regret to announce that we will be making some slight cut-backs to a few of your favourite programmes. <u>Steptoe and Son</u> will become <u>Steptoe and Cat</u>, and Wendy Craig will appear in a new series of <u>And Mother Makes One</u>, and there will also be special economy episodes of <u>The Likely Lad</u>, <u>Monty Python's Flying Puppet Show</u> and <u>The Goody</u>. <u>24 Hours</u> will become <u>45 minutes</u> and <u>News at Ten</u> will be brought forward to half past nine, so that we can close down earlier. BBC 1 will merge with BBC 2 and become BBC 1½.

Yours, Ex Controller
(I've just been made Redundant)

Luxury Goods

Buy British . . . We will make it illegal to buy anything you really want that was not made in Britain. This especially applies to Japanese cameras, TVs etc. and to German cars.

The Quality of British Workmanship

Britain has always been famed for the high quality of its products. We feel this is a prime cause of our problems. We intend to make sure that British craftsmen turn out a load of rubbish. Workers will then stop demanding more money, because there'll be nothing worth buying. British workers can then concentrate on producing the bare essentials of life, which brings us to:

Increased Productivity
& a New Form of Income Tax

We intend to entirely revise the basic principle of income tax.

In future, the *less* you earn, the *more* tax you will pay. The advantage is obvious. No-one wants to pay a lot of tax, so you will want to earn a lot to avoid being taxed. You will not earn a lot unless you work hard, and if you work hard the country will enjoy increased productivity. People who don't earn any money will have to pay very high taxes, so they'll have to work hard to be able to afford them. Once they have earned a lot, they won't have to pay the taxes after all — won't that be a nice surprise!

NEW SCALE OF INCOME TAX	EARNINGS*	£0·00	£500·01	£1001·03	£2500·04	£5000·03½	£10,216·07	£20,000·00½	over £20,000·00½
	TAX*	£15,000	£11,000·02	£6,500·06	£2500·04	£1001·02	£520·01	£0·10½	£0·00

PART 3

INCENTIVES & REWARDS

GOODY 1 BOND

Now we've got everyone working harder and earning lots of money, and there's nothing worth buying, people might as well save – can't be bad, can it! On the other hand, there's not much point in saving money if there's nothing worth buying. So, you exchange your money for Goody Bonds – £20 buys a whole bond!

WHAT'S THE POINT OF A GOODY BOND?

1 *We* get your money (which goes into the Government's account, of course).
2 You get lots of Goodies, or to be more precise, you use your Goody Bonds to pay for a holiday* – and, since you've been working so hard, you're going to need one!!

BUT NOT ANY OLD HOLIDAY....YOU CAN ENJOY

*Goody Bonds may only be used to pay for a Goody Holiday. They are otherwise valueless.

THE GOODIES' ADVENTURE HOLIDAY IN BEAUTIFUL, FASCINATING BRITAIN

Think of the advantages:
✳ *no language problems*   ✳ *no foreign food to make you throw up*
✳ *no travel to make you sick*   ✳ *no peeling skin*   ✳ *and the unique chance to indulge your special interest.*

Fancy yourself as an artist? Paint away to your heart's content.

TWO WEEK'S PAINTING ON THE PICTURESQUE FORTH BRIDGE.**

6 GOODY BONDS

EXPLORE BRITAIN'S CANALS WITH YOUR OWN BARGE.**

5 GOODY BONDS – cut rates for family parties.

Discover London on a Busman's Holiday.

DRIVE A REAL LONDON BUS AND ALL ITS PASSENGERS FOR THREE WEEKS.**

FROM AS LITTLE AS **7 GOODY BONDS

POTHOLERS!

ENJOY THREE WEEKS' MINING IN THE WELSH PITS. MILES OF UNDERGROUND TUNNELS. A SUBTERRANEAN WONDERLAND!**

4 GOODY BONDS

This is where you'll stay – one of these charming cottages (soap inclusive) will be yours for your holiday.

Fond of Animals? Get back to nature – spend two weeks at a real working farm ....**

5 GOODY BONDS

AND MANY MORE

PART 4

SELF-HELP

But we still need to economize – how can you help ? Well, our motto is help yourself. Every year millions of pounds are spent on public services – we want to make many public services *really* public: we want the public to perform them ! That means you. So, next time you are about to spend public money, think first: *Can I help myself ?* Here is just an example of what we mean:

DOCTORS ARE  EXPENSIVE

★ It takes a great deal of money to pay doctor's salaries.

★ Top surgeons demand huge fees. Everytime you are ill, you cost the National Health Service more than we can afford. You can't (though you could try) stop yourself being ill.

BUT YOU CAN # HELP YOURSELF!

Next time you need treatment, don't bother the National Health Service.

Treat yourself and check in at England's first
SELF-SERVICE HOSPITAL

AND

IT'S NEVER TOO LATE TO HELP YOURSELF.
Only you know how you really feel. Reckon you won't make it ? Are you about to snuff it ? You can't take it with you. So give your money to HM Government, and save on funeral expenses by helping yourself :

Dig own grave.

2 Pile earth onto hinged table. Tie hinged table to neck. Hold packet of daisy seeds. Wait . . .

3 Die. Fall in grave. Hinged table tips in earth. Hold onto daisy seeds.

4 Nicely buried.

5 Push up daisies

PART 13

CONSERVING ENERGY

ELECTRICITY
Home generators

Here are simple ways in which you can produce your own electricity by utilizing your own energy, and stop wasting your government's (which it cannot afford).

The Home Generator

The weight of the diners is sufficient to bear down on the spring-jacked chairs, which in turn rotates the generating wheels, which provides perfectly adequate lighting for your dining-room. It's quite fun really, and has the added advantage that, if you're fat, you will rapidly sink under the table and be unable to reach your food — an easy and effortless method of dieting!

GRAEME GARDEN

And finally, our master plan . . .

It is a fact that Englishmen and women spend millions of pounds a year on animals. We keep them in zoos and we keep them in our homes, and always at the height of luxury. These animals are enjoying a life of utter idleness and ease. They eat countless tons of food. They inhabit comfortable dwelling places. They are stroked and pampered and called soppy names. Every year it costs this country a fortune cleaning up doggie poos. Yet all these worthless beasts give us in return is the so-called pleasure of letting us stare at them for a few hours a day. This is an appalling waste of potential power and energy. We intend to put a stop to it!

Under the Goodies' Red, White and Blue-print for a Cheaper Britain, it will become an offence to support an animal who does not put in at least six man-hours (or animal-hours) every day of useful practical service to its country (except Sundays and Walkies-days).

***NB. We do not in any way wish to denigrate the invaluable and heroic service given by many thousands of farmyard animals, many of which willingly lay down their lives (or their eggs) for the benefit of mankind. It is the molly-coddled pets we're after.

Firstly, it is proposed to evict all animals from cages and enclosures at all British zoos. We can then provide warm and comfortable accommodation for hundreds of workers, especially these immigrants used to tropical conditions. The animals will remain enclosed within the grounds and the zoos' human inhabitants can still enjoy watching them just the same, from the safety and comfort of their cages . . .

THE NEW LONDON ZOO

HOW TO GET THE MOST OU

1001 different Practical Uses.

IN THE HOME ➡

French Poodle-Mop

"Old English"
Chimney and Flu Brush

"Meow!
Lick
Lick
Lick"
"A SHAMMY
PUSSY"
Excellent for
licking clean
windows,
windscreens etc.

Live Tiger-skin Rug

'Sausage-dog' Draft exclud

Grrrr
Grrrr

A nice, cozy
high-backed
mongrel-chair

Collapsible mutt-ta

Labrad
benc
black
finish

A 'ball' of snakes has a 100 use
but, *please* – N.B. it *is* crue
cut them up into
different length

Hedgehogs – wonderful for getting out those 'difficult' stains

No

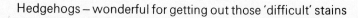

OF YOUR ANIMALS

Giraffe-poles (for Telegraph cables)

POWER AND PUBLIC SERVICE

Grapes

Parrots – daft enough to think they'll catch the grapes eventually – tee hee!

Same principle Peanuts and Bluetits

Teams of Jack Russell Terriers – save the "CHUNNEL"

"THE POLLY-COPTER"

Camel-powered Hovercraft

DOG-POWERED BUS – Problem – would need very tall dogs?

"Flap flap"

Honk!

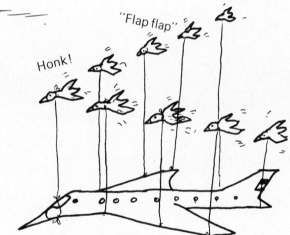

Can *Concorde* be saved?
Disadvantage–could only fly *South* in Autumn and *North* in spring!?

HE WOODPECKER ROAD-DRILL

il – use if wheels queak too much

Spare I tank"

rection vehicle

Hiss!

Direction of mice

MOUSE-WHEELED UNI-BUGGY
(Moggy-motivated)

POLICE DOGS must take a arger share of Police Duties – .e. directing traffic, etc.

And a special word on **TORTOISES** – we are very displeased with the tortoises habit of Hibernating – this is slovenly behaviour – presumably aimed at avoiding their responsibilities. In future, if tortoises continue to hibernate, they will be required – by law – to *give up their shells* – and when they are not hibernating they must live *three to a shell*.

Tortoise shells have a multitude of uses

Tortoise-shell fruit bowl

Plenty of room!

Tortoise-shell crash-helmet

Tortoise-shell ashtray

Tortoises simply do NOT NEED their shells when they are asleep.

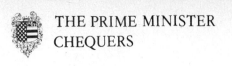

THE PRIME MINISTER
CHEQUERS

Dear Goodies,

Thanks for the 'Blue-print', lads. Some quite nice

little ideas. There may be something I can use. I'll

have a think ab...

we should pretending, as the
to imply we should, that suc...
disputes do not exist.

The more one inspects the
indictments, the more peculiar
it becomes, and the more obscure
the indications as to what we are
supposed to do about it.

Stop Press

PM's plan will save million in the next week

This photograph of the author of the New Plan was released by the Prime Minister's Press Secretary earlier today. Any guesses?

PM SAVES THE DAY!

Who is the Mystery Genius?

There were scenes of wild acclaim in the Commons when Parliament was presented with a New Plan which will undoubtedly solve the country's economic crisis.

Addressing the members, the Prime Minister made the following statement:
'This plan is a work of extraordinary foresight and genius, the product of a brilliant mind. Whoever thought of it will certainly go down in History amongst Britain's greatest heroes.'
Asked who had in fact worked out the New Plan, the Prime Minister hesitated, blushed deeply, and announced almost coyly that 'surely matters of

national importance were above the level of mere personality. It really doesn't matter *who* thought of it, what matters is that England is saved!'
There was cheering in the house as each point in the magnificent scheme was announced and members joined voices in ecstatic cries of 'Author, Author', which eventually became deafening. The Prime Minister remained his usual retiring self and

gave in only to the extent of releasing the photograph here reproduced. Naturally i... tells us nothing! And w... all feel that we know... really is magnificent, standing service to wo... of the historic duties never be forgotten beyond his wild fortune

THE SUNDAY TIMES
MARCH 23 1975
No 7919 Price 15p

Daily Mirror

THE GOODIES
No Fixed Abode, Nr. Cricklewood, London

AILY EXPRESS
Weather: Cloudy, some rain
...y April 17 1975

SENSATION – PLAN SCRAPPED

In an amazing statement in the Commons today, the Prime Minister said: 'I believe there may have been some misunderstanding about my reaction to this so-called "New Plan". I have been reported as having called it "a work of genius" – this was a slip of the tongue – I meant to say it was a "load of old cobblers". Rarely have I read such a collection of idio ideas, with no val... only lonies barmy...

Dear Sir,

You schmuch! You creep! Credit where credit's du...
All right, you play it your way and we'll play it ours...
Here's the Bill - please settle
by return post.

Invoice	
For solving economic crisis	£6,000,000.03
For working out new taxation scheme	£ 195,000.11
For doing silly drawings	£1,700,114.00½
Cost of pens, paper etc.	~~UNPAID~~
+ VAT	£ 7,000.72
at least	quite a lot
	£8,000,000.86½

THE GARDUIAN Tuesday April 15 1975

LAW REPORT

In the case of the Goddies vs Weedenfled & Nicholsno, the Jury have retired to cosnider their verdict. In a case tha thas (cont back poge col 2)

APPOINTMENTS

Miss Edith Smith, 'Daughter of Dora Smith' succeeds her mother toda yas cheif poof-readre, and we all wish her welll in her oogle-eyed serch for misprunts

Wedgwood wit
less. And yet,
thing. I mean,
nothing agai
particular tl
charm .. bu
week. Ed)
mean, its
on the
perf

THE OLD BAILEY

INSTRUCTIONS TO JURORS

The British Legal System is firmly based upon the irrevocable principle that a just and fair verdict can only be obtained from an absolutely *~~unanimous~~* decision of twelve good men and true. *majority*

You have been selected to serve as a jury member. The following instructions should be carefully read before attending the courts.

1) The jury consists of twelve members, one of whom is elected as "foreman", and who thereafter is spokesman for the jury in front of the judge.

2) You will be under the direction of the Clerk of the Court as to your conduct.

3) You must forget you ever saw "12 Angry Men."

4) Evidence will be placed before you by Learned Counsel, witnesses called and exhibits shewn, and finally the Judge will deliver his summing up. The Jury retire, and then . . .

5) It's Make-Your-Mind-Up Time!

6) At this point it is imperative that you forget about "12 Angry Men." It was a gross dramatisation of the solemn duty of a jury such as yourselves, and utterly out of keeping with the conduct of our own legal system, although Henry Fonda's performance did have the stamp of integrity so necessary to successful jury work.

7) Anyway, remember that you are judging the case on its merits. Much may depend on your decision. Your verdict, be it guilty or not guilty, or finding for the plaintiff or the defendant, may mean a great deal to those involved in the case. The responsibility could prove too much for some of you – as it did for the Ed Begley character in "12 Angry Men."

8) Do you remember the bit when one of them, Jack Warden I think, or it might have been Henry Fonda, threw the knife so it stuck in the table, and they were all amazed. That was probably one of the most powerful moments, in the film, as I am sure you would agree.

OFFICIAL COURT TRANSCRIPT
GOODIES V WEIDENFELD PUBLISHERS

DAY 95

THE JURY, HAVING SPENT THREE DAYS AND NIGHTS CONSIDERING THEIR VERDICT IN THE JURY ROOM ON THE THIRD FLOOR OF THE HOTEL MAJESTICO, THIS MORNING RETURNED TO A HUSHED COURTROOM.

CLERK OF COURT: Hush!

JUDGE: Thank you.

CLERK: Shut up . Now then – gentlemen of the jury, you will rise.

THE JURY RISES.

CLERK: Who is your foreman?

FOREMAN HOLDS UP HIS HAND.

JUDGE: You are the foreman of this jury?

FOREMAN: Yes, I know.

CLERK: Shut up.

JUDGE: Sorry.

CLERK: All right.....(MUTTERS) <u>this</u> time ....

JUDGE: Foreman of the jury, what is your verdict?
Do you find for the plaintiff or the defendant?

FOREMAN: The plaintiff.

JUDGE: You find for the Goodies?

FOREMAN: Oh...sorry, in that case we find for the defendant.

JUDGE: Sure?

FOREMAN: ....no?

JUDGE: All right I know this defendant and plainfift nonsense is ...... paintift...plaintiff...plaintiff?... yes plaintiff. Look, let's make it easier for all of us. Guilty or not guilty?

FOREMAN: Oh...not guilty.

JUDGE: Innocent?

FOREMAN: Innocent ...er...with guilty connections.

MR. ODDIE: Just a minute! This trial is a mockery!
CLERK: Well of course it is! Mr Weidenfeld wouldn't buy it if there weren't a few laffs.

JUDGE: What do you mean, Trevor?

CLERK: Look, I've sold the publishing rights on this trial to Weidenfeld and Nicolson, and...

MR.GARDEN: (LEAPING TO HIS FEET) Aha!

JUDGE: Pardon.

MR.GARDEN: Granted. I thought it was Counsel for the Defendant. However, may I submit that this trial proves our case? If these disreputable publishers are prepared to print the lies that have been told about us in this court case, then that proves that they have committed Libel against us!

JUDGE: True. But only if it is published!

MR WEIDENFELD: (RISING) Oh but it has been.

JUDGE: Wot?

MR.W.: Oh yes, it was published last week.

JUDGE: All of it? Even this bit?

MR.W.: Yep. Page 96. Auf veeder zain.(LEAVES COURT)

JUDGE: This is all most confusing. It now appears that this trial must be admiited as evidence. We are Exhibit "M".

MR B-Taylor: You're the judge, for heaven's sake! How can the judge be a (DELETED) exhibit?

JUDGE: Look sunshine, I can be whatever I (DELETED) want!

A LITTLE TITTER RAN AROUND THE COURTROOM. SQUEALS FROM SOME OF THE LADIES.

CLERK: Actually you can't, Ian, because......

JUDGE: What the (DELETED) do you know? Eh?

CLERK: Ian, a Judge can't be evidence!

JUDGE: I can so too!!

CLERK: Not in a case he's trying himself. That's ridiculous.

JUDGE: All right, Trevor, that may well be ridiculous to you, but as far as I'm concerned it's not so much a matter of being out of

(continued on page one)